The Living Word

Also by Harold Klemp:

The Book of ECK Parables, Volume 1
The Book of ECK Parables, Volume 2
Child in the Wilderness
How to Find God
Journey of Soul
The Secret Teachings
Soul Travelers of the Far Country
The Wind of Change

This book has been authored by and published under the supervision of the Living ECK Master, Sri Harold Klemp. It is the Word of ECK.

The
Living Word

Harold Klemp

Illuminated Way Publishing

P.O. Box 27088 · Golden Valley, MN 55427-0088 · 612-546-8999

The Living Word

Copyright © 1989 ECKANKAR

The terms ECKANKAR, ECK, EK, 🕮 , MAHANTA, SOUL TRAVEL, and VAIRAGI, among others, are trademarks of ECKANKAR, P.O. Box 27300, Minneapolis, MN 55427 U.S.A. and are used with its permission.

Printed in U.S.A.
Library of Congress Catalog Card Number: 89-86022

ISBN: 0-88155-083-3

Illustrations by Connie Kassal
Cover photograph by Luanne Lawton

First Printing — 1990

To All Who Love God

Contents

Preface

This book is a collection of my articles in the *Mystic World* and the *ECK Mata Journal* from 1982–88. From the very first, I envisioned these articles compiled in a single place.

The Living Word is for aspirants and students of ECK alike, for both personal reading and spiritual discussion classes. It is for all who have reached or gone beyond the no-man's-land that lies between their church and the spiritual teachings of ECKANKAR. What do the orthodox religions no longer teach that is the foundation of spiritual growth? The Sound and Light of God.

These seven years of articles are arranged in an order that begins with the introductory ECK teachings and runs to the more esoteric ones of God-Realization.

It is well to know about the Sound and Light of God, but how does a person take such knowledge and experience into his everyday life? Does God ask a lover of truth to hide away from the world of responsibility? Or can he, without fanfare, be a carrier of divine love and power to friends and neighbors?

If the reader uncovers only a tenth of the love within these pages, he will be transformed into a nobler state of being, many times over.

In the Light and Sound of ECK, read and know.

With Spiritual Blessings,
Harold Klemp

Across from me on this isolated trail stood the ancient
ECK Master Rebazar Tarzs.

1

The Living Word

The thought had been gnawing at me how ferociously some ECK chelas cling to past Masters in hopes of spiritual liberation. I wondered if they truly understood that liberation depends upon the Mahanta, the Living ECK Master. He is the Living Word.

The wind burned my face within the hooded pale blue *chuba,* a flowing gown of heavy cloth that was well suited for the harsh Tibetan climate. Across from me, on this isolated trail along a narrow mountain ridge, stood the ancient ECK Master Rebazar Tarzs. He also wore a chuba, but one of deep red instead of the knee-length maroon robe usually associated with him. Rugged leather boots guarded his feet against the sharp stones.

He read my unspoken concern and said, "In *The Shariyat-Ki-Sugmad,* bible of ECKANKAR, it is written: 'The God-intoxicated Soul who is the Living ECK Master combines in his person all that the scriptures contain and much more besides. He is the living embodiment of all that is religious, the spirit of life lying dormant in others.' "

An eagle circled high in the gray afternoon sky. Rebazar walked to the edge of the cliff on which the trail ran, the gusts of wind tearing at his robe, which he had fastened with a cloth belt. He stood on the heights as unruffled as a pedestrian on a busy street corner, waiting for the traffic light to change.

This meeting with Rebazar Tarzs had come about through the Spiritual Exercises of ECK. They are mainly for Soul to go home to God but may also be used for service and communication. My body was asleep in bed in the United States, but in the Soul body I could move through the barriers of time and space to meet Rebazar in this remote part of Tibet. The spiritual exercises let one Soul Travel, one of the first talents that ECK Masters develop in their rise to Mastership.

"Do chelas always get stuck on the personality of a Master after he leaves them?" I asked.

His dark brown eyes burned into mine. "The most dynamic expression of the ECK is always now, in this moment. Memories of It are of no use to one who walks the living path to God. Some initiates in my day felt that the expression of the Mahanta during the service of Fubbi Quantz was greater than in mine. It's like the mistaken idea that a son sired in a man's old age is weaker than his brothers."

"From what I see," I said, "once a master finishes his mission and leaves the earth, his disciples immediately drift from the precepts he gave them. Is this true of every master and his chelas?"

"The disciples of any saint are always getting off the track to God," said Rebazar, his dark eyes flashing as he seemed to watch an invisible movie screen of past history. "On the last journey of Jesus into Jerusalem, before his passion, his disciples argued about which of them were worthy to be seated beside him in heaven. He reminded them that greatness is not in authority or position, but in service to God."

2

He waved his hand for me to come to the dangerous edge of the trail and pointed to a distant caravan of yaks being herded by traders on a lower trail. The yaks moved so ponderously slow that I wondered at the patience of the men driving them.

"Until man gets spiritual freedom," said the Tibetan, "he is like the yak, a beast of burden compelled to go up and down steep mountain paths. Heavy baggage is on his back, and everything he does is under the restricting hand of karma. He is whipped by life into rebellion against it, but rebellion is repaid with greater loads, which are to tame his wild and selfish spirit."

Turning from the merchants' caravan below, Rebazar walked ahead on the narrow trail to a sharp turn which gave shelter from the ripping wind.

"Disciples of any master are continually tested in their faith to him," he said. "When Jesus was bound and sent to Caiaphas, Peter got into the palace of Caiaphas and mingled with the crowd. When asked if he knew Jesus, Peter denied all knowledge of his lord, even with curses.

"The saints of the Living Word, who are the true Godmen, have always been those who were the Mahanta, the Living ECK Master in their time. The chelas of a departed Living ECK Master seldom met his successor because of the difficulties of travel. But the Mahanta travels widely so that all who are ready for the experience of God shall have it. For this reason, I came to America in order to be among the Indians for a while."

It was late in the afternoon by now, and the sun had already crept behind the range of mountain peaks to the west. Soon this visit would end: Dawn was ready to break on the West Coast of America, where my physical body was getting a night of rest.

3

Rebazar frowned into the icy breath of the wind that now licked oftener around the shelter of the cliff's wall. "Only in ECK is there a renewal of the divine Word of the SUGMAD, or God. The Mahanta is the Living Word who gives the ever-new truth to the seeker. Who else has truth? The priests?"

His laugh was hollow above the howling of the savage wind. "No, not the priests," he said. "Early Christianity grew out of the teachings of Jesus, a student of the ECK Master Zadok. Jesus got the Second Initiation from Fubbi Quantz at the Katsupari Monastery during a three-year stay from his journeys.

"Christianity today little resembles the religion of the first century after Christ. Church services on Sunday were not required, or even on Saturday, until the time of Constantine the Great—three hundred years later. Its symbols and holy days are borrowed from the pagans. The painting of the Madonna and Child were fashioned after the Egyptian nature goddess, Isis, and the infant, Horus."

The cold evening air crept into my robe, even though the wind had let up in the last few minutes. Rebazar's darkly tanned face was still clearly visible despite the failing light.

"When the founder or guiding light of an orthodox teaching leaves the earth," he said, "his disciples carry on his message with their impure understanding. The master's instruction is later molded to fit the motives of priests who succeeded the disciples and who made themselves the caretakers of authority. Without the presence of their master to keep the original form of the teachings, his successors, who are in the human state of consciousness, corrupt them.

"Since the departed master can no longer decide religious issues for his followers, they are left to their

4

own devices. Important matters of doctrine are left to councils, which turn the master's words into a system of orthodox regulations.

"Nestorius, the Christian patriarch of Constantinople, was made a heretic by a decree of the third general council in Ephesus in 431 A.D. because he refused to acknowledge Mary as the mother of God. The distinction he made between the human and divine natures of Christ were a threat to the value of Christ's suffering and death as it was developing as a doctrine in the early church."

Rebazar had hidden his hands from the cold in the long sleeves of the chuba. "The church fathers knew that if Christianity was to become a world religion," he said, "it had to be put into a systematized form. When the bishops made a critical study of the evolving doctrines, they found they all had different interpretations about the cardinal issues of Christianity. The disputes that arose from these conflicting viewpoints led to serious arguments that almost destroyed the church.

"Much as the priestcraft deny it, Christ's teachings are no longer contained in any one church today, although each branch of Christianity teaches that it is the purest religion."

I shivered in the cold, grateful to return soon to the warm comfort of my bed at home, but I said, "Can a chela ever know the unconditional love of the Mahanta for him?"

"He can," said the Tibetan, "but only when he turns everything over to the Mahanta—all hopes, dreams, fears, and desires. The tears of Soul lead to a deep and final cleansing which brings upliftment and release: spiritual liberation."

The ancient Adept put up his right hand, palm outward, the salutation of the Vairagi Adepts. He walked off into the darkness, his light footsteps lost in the now-gentle murmur of the wind.

The Shariyat-Ki-Sugmad says: "Love comes to one in whom the Word has stirred. It is like the rushing of the mighty winds and the tongues of fire. This message of love is translated from the Word of the SUGMAD to all the universes and to every living being."

Seconds later, I stretched my rested body upon the bed on the West Coast, rubbing sleep from my eyes and quite ready for a new day.

Common sounds of ECK include the single note of a flute, a heavy wind, the music of woodwinds, even the buzzing of bees.

2

When Religion Fails Her Children

It has been said that the mark of an educated man is his resistance to new ideas. A better saying is that the spiritual seeker keeps an open mind to all knowledge. King Solomon supposedly remarked, "There is no new thing under the sun."

Therefore, one might expect a common knowledge among church people regarding the mysterious laws of Divine Spirit. This is not a sermon about etheric concepts of God. But, frankly, how many people who go to church regularly can describe in graphic terms either the Light or Sound of God?

Has religion thus failed her children? Several questions beg an answer: What is Soul? What happens to It upon death of the physical body? Is there life hereafter?

In 1965, a man named Paul Twitchell began to give public lectures about Divine Spirit and the violation of Its laws that binds every man, woman, and child to fear, misery, and despair through ignorance of them. He conducted small workshops in southern California designed to bring sincere truth seekers in touch with their spiritual identities. On the agenda was a description of

Soul and how an ordinary person could move into states of ecstatic alertness the natural way without drugs. He further gave an explanation for the troubles and cares that burdened his audience.

Among the topics were Spirit, or ECK (the Cosmic Light and Music of God); karma; and reincarnation. In appearance, Paul Twitchell was an unimposing man. Of medium height, he wore ordinary business suits and was clean shaven. Only his message was startling: "Man can enter the kingdom of heaven while still living in the human body."

Imagine what this would mean, if true: Man would be liberated from the terrors of death. He would take his place among the great spiritual travelers of history: Rama, Krishna, Pythagoras, Rebazar Tarzs, Plato, and Jesus.

As Soul, we preserve our identity throughout eternity. The Eastern religions wrongly believe that Soul becomes one with God. Rather, It becomes a Co-worker with God, fulfilling Its destiny as a citizen of the heavenly and physical worlds at the same time.

Henry Wadsworth Longfellow, the most popular American poet in the nineteenth century, knew that Soul was eternal. In "A Psalm of Life," he sings:

> Tell me not, in mournful numbers,
>   Life is but an empty dream!
> For the soul is dead that slumbers,
>   And things are not what they seem.
>
> Life is real! Life is earnest!
>   And the grave is not its goal;
> Dust thou art, to dust returnest,
>   Was not spoken of the soul.

The key to spiritual liberation is found in several simple spiritual techniques. "The Easy Way" is found in

Brad Steiger's *In My Soul I Am Free,* a biography of Paul Twitchell. Twitchell was charged by the spiritual hierarchy to deliver to the public of the modern age the teachings of ECKANKAR. In book and lecture he dealt with the realization of God's Light and Sound as well as actual experience in the other worlds in a safe manner.

An illustration of this comes in a letter from a resident of Iowa. "When I started in ECKANKAR and learned of the spiritual exercises, the Light came in after just a few weeks of practice. After the Second Initiation, the Sound came in and is ... always with me, at my job, at sleep, at play. I wouldn't have believed it three years ago if someone had explained this to me then. Experience is the best proof of the truth of the ECK."

Paul Twitchell gives "The Easy Way" technique like this: "Just before going to bed at night sit in an easy chair or on the floor, back erect, and concentrate the attention on the Spiritual Eye, that place between the eyebrows, while chanting the AUM, or God, inwardly and silently. Hold the attention on a black screen in the inner vision, and keep it free from any pictures if at all possible. If you need a substitute for any mental pictures flashing up unwantedly, place the image of Christ, or some saint, or a holy man that you know, in place of them.

"After a few minutes of this, suddenly there will come a faint clicking sound in one ear, or the sound of a cork popping, and you will find yourself outside the body looking back at the physical one in the room, and ready for a short journey in the other worlds.

"There is nothing to fear, for no harm can come to you while outside the body, nor to it when left behind. A teacher or guru will be standing by, although you may not know it, to keep watch over your progress. After a while the spirit body will return and slide gently into the body with hardly more than a very light jolt.

"If not successful the first time, try it again, for the technique works. It has worked for others."

The true goal of this is to reach the Kingdom of Heaven. The seeker undertakes a study of Divine Spirit, which is called the Word in Saint John's Gospel. This is the Voice of God. It is more powerful than the sermon of an evangelist. Spirit, or ECK, as It is known among the spiritual giants, is actually the essence of God that binds all life together. It is the golden thread that underlies all creation and all history.

"The Easy Way" is one of a series of spiritual exercises that has proved successful in man's search for God Consciousness.

The Light seen by the apostles at Pentecost is still seen today by students of the ancient teachings of ECKANKAR. So is the Sound. The apostles heard It as "a rushing mighty wind." Light and Sound show up in numerous ways, according to *The Spiritual Notebook* by Paul Twitchell, a veteran traveler of the Far Country, those planes of existence beyond this physical world. Common sounds include the single note of a flute, a heavy wind, the music of woodwinds, even the buzzing of bees. The Sound is of special importance in that it brings spiritual liberation. Man is lifted above the human consciousness into the higher realms of being. There he sheds forever the terror of death.

This individual tells of her experience with Spirit. "ECK has been in my life since 1968 when I first read *The Tiger's Fang*. It was then the Sound came to me. It seemed natural. After all, Paul Twitchell said it would! The Sound has changed now and has become more like a buzzing. It's with me all the time."

The simplest explanation is that the Voice of God, or the Sound, carries out the purification that lifts Soul to God. This is done through an agent known as the Inner Master, which can be the face of the saint placed before you during "The Easy Way." The guide stands by to help the neophyte in his own efforts toward enlightenment. Never will he intrude or interfere in any way with the will of the student without clear permission.

The illuminated way of the inner planes operates by way of the dream state, the Inner Master, and eventual contact with Spirit Itself—in the form of Light and Sound.

A young man from the midwestern United States relates his encounter with a blue light during his daily contemplation. "A few days ago," he writes, "I was in contemplation. At some point the realization came to me that I was awash in a blue light. It would fade out at times, only to return more strongly. Sometimes its intensity was brighter than a powerful electric light. It flowed and swirled around me. Soon it had become a brilliant tunnel, and I was rushing, and yet not rushing, down it. At the end of the tunnel a brilliant blue-white light like a diamond was awaiting me. After a while the vision faded away."

There is a similarity in the description of the Sound of ECK from a housewife in Missouri. "I hear the Sound Current almost constantly. Buzzing of the bees, symphony of the winds, now and then the flute. But always the Sound."

In the mixed-up world of nuclear threat, uncontrolled diseases, and an uncertain economy, there is a sanctuary. Health and wealth do not bring joy and peace. Only the realization of God can do it.

No sensible person dives headlong into something as important as ECKANKAR. I urge inquirers to first read several ECK books. This ought to take several months to a few years. During that interval, you will certainly know whether this is the answer to your quest.

One oddity among people who look for either Self- or God-Realization is that they believe they are excused from personal responsibility for their actions. The divine laws are for others, never themselves. Thus in ignorance, they break them and pay dearly into the coffers of the Lords of Karma. The path of ECK teaches these laws. It is the path of total responsibility and freedom.

When you come to the point where religion fails in its answers and you throw up your hands to Spirit, as did a friend of mine—"What more do you want from me, perfection?"—then you are ready to see the holy fire of ECK.

If you are an explorer who knows "that there is no new thing under the sun," you are ready to walk the high road traveled by untold thousands before you. Step into the fresh, new worlds of ECK!

The palace auditorium was crowded with ambassadors from every religion. One hesitant voice asked, "Your lordship, what is meant by 'Light and Sound'?"

3

What the Old Religions Forgot
Kal Gets a Message from Sat Nam

The order had come from headquarters, so what could he do?

Kal Niranjan, the lord of material creation, angrily paced his office. Seldom did he get directives from Sat Nam, but when he did, they turned his universal network upside down. As ruler of the Atma Lok, the first of the pure positive God Worlds, Sat Nam is lord of all the worlds below.

Niranjan was above average in height, fleshy from too much food and wine and partying. He looked like the chief executive of a major corporation, rather than the commander-in-chief of all the worlds below the spiritual planes. In his hand was a message just received by the communications department. It read:

Make a performance review of the old religions. Are they still productive? What are their present operating procedures? Do any still teach the Light and Sound of God? Report to me a week from today.

> *Sat Nam*
> *Agent for the SUGMAD*
> *Atma Lok*

17

The next morning the palace auditorium was crowded with ambassadors from every religion one could think of. The dress of the representatives reflected every culture. Before the start of the session, people were milling about the Great Hall, eyeing each other with suspicion. A conclave like this had not been called together in several thousand years, and the buzzing in the crowd expressed an anxious concern of what new erratic mandate would issue from the Kal Niranjan, king of the negative power.

There is no need to go into the names of those religious teachings that are unknown to us on earth. It should be noted, however, that the old principle "As above, so below" means that the diversity of religions on earth are only reflections of those religions that preexisted on the invisible planes above. The earth religions are corruptions of the already diluted ones that exist in the inner worlds.

Roll was called. Leaders of denominations raised their hands when the name of their splinter group was read. These included the subdivisions of animism, ancestor worship, polytheism, dualism, monotheism, supratheism, pantheism. August representatives of these old religions solemnly nodded to the chairman as the spotlight of attention briefly flitted upon their institutional group.

Judaism, Christianity, Hinduism, Islam, Buddhism, Brahmanism, and Taoism acknowledged their presence. Among the Christians, the Baptists, Catholics, Episcopalians, Lutherans, Fundamentalists, Quakers, Presbyterians, Congregationalists, and other denominations fluffed their feathers in turn.

The roll call took the better part of the day, and a recess was taken until the next morning.

After an early breakfast, the Kal Niranjan occupied a large stage set in the middle of the auditorium. Suspended from the ceiling above him in a circle were eight giant screens that showed his greatly magnified image to every person in the hall. His voice thundered over the sound system:

The great lord Sat Nam has sent down an order to all religions. This is the age to bring a fuller knowledge of the Light and Sound of God to the awareness of Souls in every corner of the universes.

Gasps of consternation filled the hall. Ambassadors turned to each other, shrugging their shoulders and rolling their eyes heavenward. Whispers hummed throughout the hall until the sound became like a shushing wind in the autumn leaves.

A hesitant voice broke the wave of perplexity washing through the Great Hall. The official from a Roman Catholic splinter group had gotten up courage to address the fearsome Niranjan. He spoke for the assembly.

"Your lordship, begging your pardon, in reverence I respectfully request, What is meant by 'Light and Sound'?"

Heads nodded vigorously throughout the hall, and the Kal Niranjan was quick to note this. The question was an honest one and not an attempt to threaten his seat of power.

The meeting had reached a sudden stalemate. Niranjan had no idea what the phrase meant and, apparently, neither did any of the leaders of the major religions. The only group of people that seemed to have any idea of Sat Nam's "Light and Sound" directive was a small pocket of representatives in the mystical-religion part of the hall. He adjourned the main meeting until the next day and immediately held a meeting with only the heads of the major groups, plus a few of those among the mystical religions. The object was to sift through the early history of the universal religion, before it had begun to split off into a multitude of splinter groups, and find references to the Light and Sound of God.

Frankly, the Christian leaders were the most puzzled of all. As the Catholic and Protestant leaders agreed: There is a communion, baptism, sin, the Ten Commandments, the Golden Rule, but nowhere could they find any clues to the Light and Sound of God that could be controlled or used in the administration of their institutions. Furthermore, they knew about the tongues of fire experienced by the apostles at Pentecost, and the sound as of a rushing wind, but those phenomena had pretty much stopped with the passing of primitive Christianity.

The mystical religions were a little more help. Most of them were located in India, with offshoots in obscure forms around the world. They indeed taught the Light and Sound, but only a few of their followers actually had any personal experience with It. This was the first real lead that the Kal Niranjan found about the Light and Sound of God. Maybe he would be able to carry out the unbendable mandate from Sat Nam to bring knowledge of them to Souls in all the worlds.

But the mystical leaders proved to be of little real help. The convention ended after five days, and a report was sent to the supreme headquarters of Sat Nam on the Soul Plane. It is too long to quote here in its entirety, but a summary of it goes like this:

A universal investigation has failed to turn up any information that can implement a teaching program of the Light and Sound of God. All levels of consciousness in my control were examined for even minute traces of

20

what seems to be an ancient teaching that is lost to our historians. Can you advise?

> *Kal Niranjan*
> *Manager of the Mental Worlds*
> *and All Below*

A few short hours passed before the communication center stirred with frenzied activity. Messages from Sat Nam came on rare occasions, once every few millennia or so. Therefore, the operators had their receiving equipment tuned to the most sensitive settings. The printers were adjusted to catch the message in the clearest possible manner.

Sat Nam's note was indirect and disconcerting. While it did not chide the Kal, it was mysterious about his role in implementing the original order to propagate information about the Light and Sound of God. He was strangely troubled as he read the note, not so much for what it said, but for what it didn't say. The note in full:

You have done what you could. This program will be explored more fully in my office. There are plans to implement this program in a test case. The old religions are found to be too entangled in social conventions to be fit conveyors of the ancient teachings of the SUGMAD. A new outlet will be established to set this desire of the SUGMAD into motion. Back to business as usual.

> *Sat Nam*
> *Agent for the SUGMAD*
> *Atma Lok*

Before his response, Sat Nam had set up an investigative panel, which came to the conclusion that the old religions were too embedded in the traditions of the social consciousness to be able to serve as carriers for the pure Light and Sound of God. The Order of Vairagi Adepts, under the guidance of such notables as Rebazar Tarzs, Fubbi Quantz, and Yaubl Sacabi—expert field agents—deemed it best to carry out this mission through the pure spiritual channels and bypass the Kal Niranjan's hierarchy entirely. Rebazar Tarzs, who was then the Mahanta, the Living ECK Master, the head of the Vairagi Order, proposed to train a certain Peddar Zaskq for implementing this plan of the SUGMAD. The idea met with complete approval.

Several centuries passed as Peddar Zaskq was made to take on a number of incarnations to bring about the spiritual polishing needed for the job. He was born into his latest life as Paul Twitchell in the early part of this century. A variety of professions, including those of writer, promoter, and military man, were the furnaces that tempered his rebellious nature to fit him for the special mission of bringing the Light and Sound of God to people at all levels of consciousness.

The vehicle he created to carry out this mission was called ECKANKAR. It has met violent opposition from contemporary religions because it is not a part of the Kal Niranjan's system of religious education. Being an alien doctrine—a spiritual one of purity among those of power struggles—it has met fierce opposition.

It has been adjudged a heretical doctrine, its people subjected to the embarrassment of what can only be called the Medieval Rites of Inquisition. Even in the United States, ECKists, whose great-grandparents settled America, are treated like illegal immigrants slipping from Haiti into Florida. The consciousness of the general population is quite low, despite the vaunted advances of science, which have done nothing to raise the human consciousness. Essentially, middle-class

America is Medieval Europe with a new face. The problem is rooted in the absence of something—something forgotten by the old religions.

What the old religions forgot is the Light and Sound of God.

The purpose of ECKANKAR is therefore to put It back into the consciousness of man. The spiritual view of God is the only way to a new golden age in the life of mankind.

What the old religions forgot, ECKANKAR has restored.

A schoolboy wrote that he sees a dot of blue which becomes large enough to encompass him and the Master who "pops out of nowhere and takes me places."

4

The Hidden Treasure

For centuries, religious devotees explored remote cultures hoping to unmask the face of God. In recent years this led many travelers on sacred pilgrimages to India. Man sought relief from the anguish of loneliness, despair, anxiety, and the fear of death.

It was hardly surprising, in retrospect, to find that many of these searches for real illumination ended in dismal failure. Who could be found to reveal the treasure of the Light and Sound of God? Truth has been hidden by those who wish to make slaves of the masses, says *The Shariyat-Ki-Sugmad,* the golden scriptures of ECKANKAR.

The Hindus mistakenly claim that Soul becomes one with God. The ECKist knows that the mission of every God-Realized individual is to be a Co-worker with God, for in no sense does Soul merge with God. Rather, It becomes one with Spirit and retains Its own individuality, moving into ever-higher states of consciousness unknown to man's religions.

A lady informed Paul Twitchell, the spiritual leader of ECKANKAR until 1971, that she was going to India to find a great sage who could give her the secrets of life.

"Don't go," he advised her. An enormous struggle racked her mind. Was this articulate man, who was always dressed in some sort of blue clothing, really the Mahanta? Had he actually attained God Consciousness?

She gambled that he had, and she stayed home. During the next few years the decision proved justified, for the Mahanta helped her establish herself in the Soul body where she gained spiritual liberation. This was done through the Sound and Light of God.

One of the most striking records in print today about the Sound and Light, the twin pillars of God, is *The Tiger's Fang,* authored by Paul Twitchell. The book's history has been marked by controversy since its publication in 1967. Throughout his varied writings, Paul Twitchell stated that man must first find the Light and Sound before he can discover the unique revelations of God.

 What importance do Sound and Light bear for the truth seeker? First of all, God expresses ITSELF as a visible and audible wave, similar to a radio wave broadcast from a radio transmitter. This wave is the ECK, known as Spirit, the divine power that supports and sustains all creation. Soul, the spark that God has placed in the human form, catches this wave and rides it back into the Kingdom of God.

As a child, my attitude toward God was set in fear. Practically every Sunday morning, Grandma chastised Dad for our late arrival at church. "The Lord will lock the gates of heaven," she stormed from her backseat-driver's position in our old Dodge. That reinforced my terror of hell, especially when a summer thunderstorm happened to strike during church services: My father, as if to purposely vex an already overwrought God, slept peacefully through the sermon despite the onslaught of wind and rain pelting against the stained-glass windows. This dread lingered throughout my youth. Years later, after ECKANKAR had entered my life, the fear gradually subsided as I gained seasoning through the Spiritual Exercises of ECK.

The Tiger's Fang was the first book about the intriguing subject of ECKANKAR that I read. The orderly progression of the heavens sketched therein rang true, yet what if it was only a highly imaginative science-fiction novel?

Shortly after starting the spiritual exercises I knew better, and there followed the halting steps of the apprentice. But as my insights grew, so did my trust in the purpose and justness of life. Brad Steiger recounted my initial encounter with the Inner Master in his biography of Paul Twitchell, *In My Soul I Am Free.*

I sincerely wanted to find the path of ECK easy, magically smooth, adorned with a royal carpet, and strewn with roses. The deep secrets of Spirit, however, are revealed only to the person who has earned the right to reach into the very heart of God.

My early groping for truth excluded these twin aspects of Spirit. My childhood religion was not aware of their importance in the spiritual life of the parishioner.

In vain I struggled through volumes of books on astrology, handwriting analysis, water dowsing, numerology, magic, ancient histories like *Popul Vuh,* accounts by so-called holy men detailing their achievements in personal growth, and even astral travel. Countless libraries yielded up their treasures as I hounded the elusive trail to God, but each thread of hope dried up like a lake cut off from a life-giving stream.

The Christian Bible gives but vague reference to the Sound and Light. Moses saw the Light as he tended his father-in-law's sheep. It appeared like a flame bursting from a bush, but without consuming it. Jesus recognized the Sound when he told Nicodemus, the Pharisee, that the "wind bloweth where it listeth, and thou hearest the sound thereof, but canst not tell whence it cometh, and whither it goeth." Saint John called Spirit "the Word." This is the physical manifestation of the ECK. Saul of Tarsus was rendered blind by the Light on the road to Damascus before regaining his sight three days later.

△ The Sound Current must always be the basis for the pure spiritual works, for it is the Sound and Light that brings the pure state of God-Realization.

The ECK Masters of the Ancient Order of the Vairagi have evolved a series of spiritual exercises that can lift one into the God Worlds of ECK. Among these are three specific techniques listed in *The Spiritual Notebook* by Paul Twitchell. They will work for practically anyone who is at all serious about unfolding into Self- and God-Realization. The Surat, the first, brings one the Melody of ECK. The second, the Nirat, shows the Light. The final method is the Dhyana, for it brings both the Sound and Light in the form of the Mahanta, the Inner Master.

What is it like to have this encounter with the Sound and Light of ECK? This is how one woman knew it: "Lately, during my spiritual exercises, I find myself in the center of a vibrating ECK current where pure Light and Sound are being transmitted. It is like the frequency band described for TV channels. As spiritual insights flood in, I find a new point of view on learning to be a clear channel."

The Light to the secret Kingdom of God may be any color of the rainbow, especially blue, yellow, or white. The Light shows Soul the pitfalls and obstacles on Its journey home to God. The Sound may be heard as thunder, the roar of the sea, the keen note of a flute, or even the chirping of crickets, among other sounds listed in *The Spiritual Notebook.*

A man disclosed that he put his attention on the Inner Master during contemplation. "I was sitting upright and quite conscious when this happened," he notes. "The room filled with gold, blue, and violet light and the Sound Current intensified like the buzzing of bees and an electrostatic hum, yet was different than either of these."

Does this mean that the initiate will have a constant stream of heavenly Light and Music during every waking moment? Not at all. Weeks may pass without conscious recall, for the Inner Master frequently pulls the curtain on the memory in order to maintain the student's balance. But the individual is assured that the presence of the Master is always with him at these times.

Fubbi Quantz, a monk who later became the Mahanta, the Living ECK Master during the time of Buddha, despaired when he passed through the Dark Night of Soul, thinking that God had certainly forgotten him. Wearily he dragged himself up a nearby mountain peak and unexpectedly received the Light and Sound of SUGMAD. On his return to the monastery, the other monks noticed the Light shining around his head. The old abbot in charge of the monastery let him contemplate for days in the seclusion of his cell so that he could sort out the revelations that Spirit had given to him.

The mid-twentieth century ushered in a revival of mysticism. Thomas Merton, a Trappist monk and author of *The Seven Storey Mountain,* was touched by the Light. There is no indication, however, that he ever heard the golden Music of God.

The ECKist is not a mystic, for the mystic has hardly passed the Mental worlds. This is the location of the Christian heaven, and Saint Paul referred to it as "the third heaven." The Mahanta escorts the ECKist to the true worlds of the SUGMAD which lie well beyond the Mental regions, to the Soul Plane and further. The pure worlds of God have no complication or mystery about them.

The Mahanta guided the following writer to a visit in the high heavens of God. "I awoke in the dream state to find myself in a formless world of the softest white light," he reported. "Suddenly, there appeared a white star before me. And upon seeing it, I realized I was the white star. At this point what seemed to be a river of light flowed from it to me, and I became absorbed into it. Then the light became very bright, blinding..."

The purpose of the Living ECK Master is to help each Soul find liberation from the wheel of reincarnation. It is not necessary to wait until after death to attain freedom.

Children are quite nonchalant about their experiences with Spirit, even though theirs are more substantial than many of those ascribed to mystics like Jakob Böhme, the German mystic cobbler. A schoolboy just learning to express himself by letter, recently wrote, "I see you come very fast in my dreams and spiritual exercises. First I see a little dot of blue, then it gets bigger and bigger until I am in it. Then you pop out of nowhere and take me places."

An invitation is extended to any true seeker who wants to find for himself the Light and Sound of God. This treasure is the birthright of Soul that leads to the Kingdom of Heaven.

The man appeared to her in a dream and gave her a ring with many keys on it.

5

The Sound and Light of Heaven

Teachers of contemporary religion are innocent about the nature of Soul. Missing vital experience in the higher states of consciousness via Soul Travel, they cannot speak with authority of the golden keys to heaven, the Sound and Light of God, which lead Soul to freedom.

But the ECK Masters can.

These are the wonderful travelers that the ECK, or Holy Spirit, empowers to enliven the spiritual consciousness of man: first in the dream state, then in full awareness during Soul Travel—which is simply one's expansion of consciousness through the different planes of God. They acquaint those who desire wisdom with the transcendent Sound and Light, the two features of the Holy Spirit that give life and breath to Soul.

The Mahanta, the Living ECK Master is head of this spiritual order of ECK Adepts. He sets no store by baptism, communion, or confession as practical routes to heaven. Such rituals and practices have little merit in one's pursuit of true spiritual freedom.

Spiritual travelers routinely cross the borders of life and death; they travel freely in the heavenly worlds because they are the agents of God, whom they know as the SUGMAD. These Masters are always on the go, entrusting the secret of God to anyone who sincerely wants to overcome the fear of death, gain true knowledge of God, and become a God-directed individual. He must love God more than the air he breathes before the ECK Masters will even approach him with the ECK message of spiritual liberation. They may appear at the most unexpected times, but always to give a blessing, if one is ready for it.

A certain ECKist had many important spiritual dreams since she began to study ECK. In one series of dreams, she found herself exploring the rooms of sometimes a one-storied, sometimes a two-storied apartment. She awoke with the feeling that someone had been with her, but mainly, she just wanted to know the meaning of these recurring dreams.

The spiritual traveler who had gone with her to this place was telling her that she was now beginning her journey to God. The dream image of the one-storied apartment meant that in Soul awareness she was dwelling on the first plane, the Physical Plane. The two-storied apartment indicated that her dream travels were now taking her to a higher level—one step closer to God—to the Astral Plane, which is immediately above the Physical Plane.

In another dream, an ECK Master came in the Soul body to give her a blessing. He came again later, but this time in his physical body: to consolidate her inner and outer awareness of the ECK teachings.

She had quite forgotten the dream meeting with this ECK Master, the day she rode a subway in a city on the East Coast of the United States. The car was nearly empty except for a man sitting across from her and four people on the far end. She decided to use the time to contemplate upon God and shut her eyes to silently sing HU, the sacred name of God. This word raises Soul to an awareness of the Sound and Light of the Holy Spirit, the ECK. Once an individual contacts these two qualities of God, he will never rest until entering fully into God Consciousness.

When the train pulled out from the stop before hers, the man was still in the seat opposite her. She again shut her eyes to sing HU, but when she opened them an instant later, he was gone, nowhere in sight.

His strange disappearance haunted her the rest of the day. Late in the afternoon, she suddenly realized he was the same man who had appeared to her in a recent dream. In the dream he had greeted her with the ancient blessing of the ECK Masters. "May the blessings be," he had said simply, handing her a ring with many keys on it. These were her keys to heaven, given to her because she loved God with all her heart; the holy name of HU was always on her lips.

Even today she continues to hear the divine Sound of God. She knows that God communicates to mankind through this Sound and Light. The sounds of ECK are many, but the one she heard recently was a clicking sound, which then became a medium-pitched tone that rose to an ever-higher pitch. The Sound of ECK, however It is heard, spiritually elevates anyone who is so fortunate as to hear this celestial melody. But one is twice-blessed who both hears the Sound and sees the Light.

Another time she was in contemplation, and the Light came to accompany the Sound. Her Spiritual Eye opened to a soft white light. At first she moved toward the light, but then the white light began to pour into her in huge waves. The Sound and Light were purifying her of karma, so that she would never need to return to

35

earth in the seemingly endless cycles of death and re-birth.

 Purification by Sound and Light is the only way for Soul to enter the higher kingdoms of God. Therefore, the ECK Masters endorse these two aspects of the Holy Spirit. Neither baptism nor confirmation give Soul the passkeys to the true heaven, which begins at the Soul Plane.

 In ECK, the individual is instructed in the laws of Spirit. How he uses this knowledge determines how soon he enters the joyful state of God Enlightenment, which can be attained while still in the human body.

A spiritual law, such as the Law of Silence, may be disarmingly simple on the surface, but its scope only becomes apparent when the individual tries to practice it. This particular law means to keep silent about what-ever passes between the spiritual student and the Mahanta, who is the Inner Master: unless, of course, instructed otherwise by the Master. But people tend to overlook such laws, especially if the tests are given in their own backyards.

An ECK initiate was pleased to have a number of Soul Travel experiences into the higher worlds of God. He even caught a glimpse of the Soul Plane with its great waves of white light tinged with soft yellow tones. His inner life was apparently in order, yet he had an outer problem that was almost too mundane to men-tion: deer eating his garden at night. But this outer problem was related to a misunderstanding of how the Law of Silence operates.

In trying to resolve this problem, he started out in the right direction. In contemplation, he asked the Mahanta to talk with the deer entity, who is responsible for the welfare of deer. Could the deer get their meals someplace else? This approach to the problem actually

36

did work for three weeks, during which time the deer did not violate his garden once. But then he made a mistake: he told a friend of the Mahanta's help. Just that quickly the deer returned to his garden. He was at a loss to understand why the Master's protection had been withdrawn.

It was for this reason: Whenever one makes a request of the Mahanta, a cohesive ball of causation is set into motion. The fabric of this causation can be torn apart if that private communication is confided to anyone else, and hence, the protection is gone.

If someone who loves God wants the divine melody and celestial light, he may chant HU. This is a spiritually charged word. Together, the Sound and Light provide Soul with the surest known way home to the Kingdom of God. But if one is unsuccessful with HU, he may use another term in its place, Wah Z.

The woman in the following story was new to ECK. She attended lectures and discussions on the spiritual teachings, chanted HU as directed, but this produced no conscious experiences of either Sound or Light. A friend suggested she try chanting Wah Z.

One night, just before going to sleep, she felt a strong need to chant Wah Z, which she did not then know was the spiritual name of the Mahanta, the Living ECK Master. And when she sang it, a wondrous feeling of peace came upon her; moreover, a heavenly sound drifted down over her. This startled her, but she sensed there was nothing to fear. So she relaxed to enjoy the music from heaven.

It seemed "as though a chorus of angels and every beautiful sound in the universe had combined" to reassure her that she was not alone. The music soon reached a crescendo, was in her and of her, indicating that she was in and with the Holy Spirit. This kind of spiritual experience is highly uncommon in most religions, except for secondhand reports from the lives of saints. But ECKists are quite familiar with such experiences with the Holy Spirit, because ECKANKAR is certainly the most dynamic and direct path to God on earth today.

The Sound gradually faded to where she had to strain to hear It, before It vanished completely. Yet the very essence of her room had changed, and so had she; tears of bliss and joy streamed down her face. Ever after she would hunger for that Sound, because It was the Voice of God calling her to come home.

The Sound and Light are the heart of the ECK teachings, which say that only love, and love alone, can give us the key to heaven.

<u>ECK is love, and love is all.</u>

And may the blessings be!

He had a vivid dream in which Simha, the Lady of
ECK, assured him that he was progressing well in his
spiritual unfoldment.

6

What Really Is the Word of God?

By definition, the Word of God is simply the Sound Current, or the ECK. The Bible calls It the Holy Ghost, or Holy Spirit.

It is easy to make a definition like this, but few people in the world today actually know what the ECK is or how It works. This is where ECKANKAR takes the lead in exploring the frontiers of the spiritual worlds. It is on the cutting edge of knowledge about the Holy Spirit. Research by the Living ECK Master, through the unfoldment of those who put their spiritual lives in his care, adds to what little mankind knows about this mysterious Life Force, the ECK.

The Shariyat-Ki-Sugmad, Book One, one of the sacred scriptures of ECK, describes the ECK as the creative primal force that flows from the heart of God. It is like a great wave that forever vibrates throughout all the universes.

A God-seeker must find his way to ECK and meet the Mahanta, the Living ECK Master. The latter is able to link the individual with the Sound Current, which leads to liberation from the darkness of matter. It restores the seeker to the Kingdom of God.

The Sound Current is heard as Sound and seen as Light. Whoever experiences them is established in the pure consciousness.

Case histories will be given of people who have experienced the Sound or Light. But another point bears mention: The Mahanta, the Living ECK Master is the embodiment of the ECK. Through him, Soul is lifted from the darkness of matter and mind into the splendid worlds of Light and Sound.

The scenario then is this: Soul is a spark of God. It is in the lower worlds to gain experience to become a Co-worker with God. To break the chains of karma and acquire spiritual liberation, Soul must first find the Mahanta. He is the living embodiment of the ECK and can link Soul with the Sound Current. Soul can then ride that Wave back home, into the heart of God. Thereafter, It enjoys the attributes of wisdom, power, and freedom. It can then give service to God in whatever capacity is desired.

But there must be a beginning. Soul's journey home to God begins with the final disillusionment with Its present unfoldment, which has gone stale. Then It looks for truth, giving up the old religious precepts of Its spiritual childhood. At this point the individual may have an experience with the Sound Current, which the Mahanta gives for his benefit, to awaken his Spiritual Eye.

The Mahanta may sometimes contact a person years before he comes across ECKANKAR. The latter may have no conscious recall of the Mahanta, Soul Travel, or the Sound and Light of ECK. This contact, however, is made in response to his disillusionment with old religious beliefs.

Let's look at a typical inner struggle: For ten years a certain woman belonged to a metaphysical religion.

During all that time she felt as if she had come to a dead end. It seemed that she had gone as far as possible with reality, at least in this plane of existence. What would happen to her after death remained to be seen. Perhaps nothing lay beyond death. Perhaps religion really was the great opiate of the masses. But in her heart, she did not fully believe that.

She finally took steps to remove her name from the files of the metaphysical church. All this took place before she heard of ECKANKAR.

Then she found ECK. But it was still several years before she actually heard the Sound Current for the first time. It happened at an ECK seminar in Chicago. Until then she had counted herself outside the group that would ever hear It. When she heard the Sound of God within her, she felt joy. During the intervals when It was silent, she felt empty.

This brief description of her experience gives only the barest indication of the grandeur and majesty of the Sound Current, which has the power to transform the life of an individual. It is a wave of indescribable proportions that flows from the SUGMAD (God) to all creation. It is the purifier of Soul.

This next example is of a woman who heard the Sound years before she came across the teachings of ECK. One night, as she lay awake in bed, she became aware of a sound inside her that was difficult to describe. It was like a multitude of crickets, but also like many ticking clocks. The more she listened, the louder it became. The intensity increased until it changed into a whistle, or better, into the single note of a flute. The musical sound had the peculiar ability to be inside her, yet it was also outside her.

Now the Sound began to prepare her for Soul Travel, but fear prevented her from going on with the experience. She felt herself floating outward in the Soul body. At the same time she was floating inward toward the Sound. Timidity got the best of her, and she resisted the Mahanta, who was trying to lift her into a higher state of consciousness via Soul Travel.

Today she wishes she had followed the experience to its end. After her reluctance in regard to Soul Travel, the Mahanta simply continued by other means to insure her spiritual purification.

The Shariyat-Ki-Sugmad, Book One, says that "the ECK descends and ascends in vibratory currents, producing life in all forms; producing music inherent and inborn that gives joy to the heart of those who have the power to hear Its melody."

Further, "with this comes freedom, the liberation that brings to Soul the very essence of happiness."

The other aspect of the ECK is the Light. Some people have experiences with It rather than with the Sound. It all depends upon the line of spiritual unfoldment they have chosen to follow in their past lives upon earth.

A boy of thirteen experienced the Light of God in an unusual way. One particular night a lightning bolt shot past his left shoulder. The sky was absolutely clear, so he could not understand what might have happened to him. This incident took place about the time that he began searching through books for a truth greater than that of his own religion.

Years passed. One night he and a childhood friend were sitting outside on a car. Suddenly the whole southern horizon lit up as if it were daylight. They both sat stunned for a second, then asked each other, "Did you see that?" The Mahanta was responsible for this experience, to further awaken the Spiritual Eye of Soul. No

44

one else in the area reported the unusual phenomenon of celestial light.

By and by the young man moved to another state and joined the Mormon church. During his youth he had seen occasional flashes of light, and now they began to return. He was coming closer to the day that he would find ECKANKAR. At a church meeting he tried to describe to others the Blue Light he often saw: it was about the size of a quarter and appeared at unexpected intervals. Nobody knew what he was talking about, since the Light of God was not a part of their experience.

About this time he had a vivid dream in which Simha, the Lady of ECK, appeared to him. He had just fallen asleep when he found himself standing before a blond woman. She wore a blue robe and called him her son. She assured him that he was progressing well in his spiritual unfoldment, but he was to continue his search for truth.

What astounded him was the tremendous love he felt in her presence. It was like a wave rolling across the ocean. The wave of love was the Sound Current, which was pouring out to him through the Lady of ECK. That was years ago. Since then, Divine Spirit has brought a change to his life: mainly, fear is fading away. In its stead he is developing a compassionate, yet detached, love for all living things.

Love is the sum of all. It is the missing element in many people's lives, but few know how to find it.

* * *

These are actual cases of people who have experienced the Sound and Light of God. Such people have a broad comprehension of life, because they have partaken of the Word of God. Although many claim to speak to God, an ECKist is taught to *listen* to ITS Voice. He is both the observer *and* participant, one who drinks of the Living Waters.

The way anyone can find the love of ECK is through the Spiritual Exercises of ECK. Several are included in *ECKANKAR — The Key to Secret Worlds* by Paul Twitchell. Many more exercises are in the *ECK Dream Discourses*.

Whoever wants spiritual freedom can find the way, here and now. ECK leads Soul into the arms of God.

He explained that the little column of white light she was seeing was the ECK, or Spirit.

7

The Shadow of Truth

When I first came across the path of ECK, thoroughly disillusioned with the church's doctrine of salvation, I had studied a host of literature devoted to religion and the occult. My thirst for divine knowledge had grown so great that I dedicated all free time to investigating authors who gave reports and theories about the inner worlds. Much of the information proved false, published only to provide an income for the writer.

A further examination of palm reading, astrology, numerology, and the like showed that the golden jewels of spiritual wisdom still eluded me, a treasure buried under shifting sands.

When ECKANKAR came into my life, while I served as an airman in Japan, I felt the breath of Divine Spirit stirring the currents around me. Soul had heard the thin, biting call of God and wanted to go home. Was there truth in ECKANKAR or was this another shadow of truth, like all the other religious teachings I had devoured with a frantic mind?

All paths that do not teach active participation in the Sound Current are only shadows of truth. The

49

Living ECK Master quietly steps aside, respecting the chela's decision to fall back into the lower worlds of death and reincarnation. Yet the Master will open the gateways of heaven to anyone who takes responsibility for his own actions.

Contact with Spirit often goes unnoticed because the experience is too commonplace, too much a part of one's own being. For example, a number of years ago an aspirant in a Satsang class told the Arahata that she could not see the Light. "What do you see?" the Arahata asked her.

"Only this little column of white light," she replied humbly.

The Arahata explained that this was the ECK and that everyone will contact Spirit in their own way. After she understood this, the aspirant blossomed like a flower in spring and today serves as a Higher Initiate in ECK.

A Second Initiate had her first conscious encounter with a celestial being when she was already a very old woman. Despite the Living ECK Master's attempts to help her lay a sound spiritual foundation, this experience toppled her back into the lower states of consciousness. The celestial being from the Astral Plane announced, amid a great show of magnificence, that the door to salvation and the Kingdom of Heaven was shut to all but Christian believers.

Never having met an entity from beyond the illusory veil before, the Second Initiate cowered meekly before him. Her timid steps into the vast reaches of the God Worlds lasted until her courage failed her. In the eleventh hour of life, she gambled on the religion of her youth, the teaching that gave the most comfort. Perhaps this decision was good for her. It is not for me nor anyone else to say.

Another correspondent was disappointed that he had not yet seen the Inner Master. However, two successive bright flashes of light had appeared to him during contemplation. So blinding were they that they even scared him for a moment.

In addition, he mentioned that the Sound came like bells, which rang for a few minutes and then turned into a high-pitched sound. The latter sound had been with him for years prior to ECKANKAR. He could not fathom its meaning nor could anyone enlighten him about it. Only after reading an ECK book did he know how he had been blessed by the ECK. He learned that all along he had been listening to the melody of ECK.

When the Tisra Til, or Spiritual Eye, opens, then the Light and Sound come to the Initiate. The disciple meets the Master in the Nuri Sarup, the Light body, when both these aspects of the SUGMAD converge and form a single matrix. This is the Dhyana spoken of in *The Spiritual Notebook*. The Mahanta stations himself at the Spiritual Eye in order to purify the negative thought stream that always flows into the mind, making the spiritual exercises supremely important to the chela.

Other people find something quite different when the Spiritual Eye opens. An awareness grows, not of the other worlds, but of the love and protection of the Mahanta that encircles them like the radiant heat of a tropical sun. Other individuals simply *know* that their spiritual welfare is being directed by the great hand of ECK.

Thus awakened, Soul leaves behind forever any yearning for the shadows of truth.

While investigating spiritual consciousness, Wah Z signed up for two religion classes in Askleposis, the Astral center of culture and art.

8

In Search of God

We commonly think that the ECK Masters see and know all things without the need for study or research. But they are, in fact, scientists who turn the worlds of God upside down to investigate the never-ending study of spiritual consciousness. All earlier research is double-checked and later gathered into the scriptures of the Shariyat-Ki-Sugmad.

In pursuit of such research on the inner planes, Wah Z signed up for two religion classes in Askleposis, the Astral center of culture and art. He wanted to compare the mental teachings of the orthodox religions with those of the heart, of ECK.

The first class was full of bright children and a scattering of adults who wanted a fresh approach to God. The children sat at desks in orderly rows, but the grown-ups simply sat crosslegged on the plush ivory carpet, textbooks spread on the floor in front of them. Wah Z chose a seat on the floor by the desks of three twelve-year-old girls.

Gray hair was beginning to streak the teacher's temples; he was lean, taller than Wah Z, and he walked among the desks with quick, agitated steps. His face was rather plain; nevertheless, he was a colorful character whom the children liked for his enthusiasm for teaching.

Today was to be a special lesson: the teacher would speak of God. Unfortunately, all he knew was so much mental hash—faith, baptism, communion, confirmation, and penance. The children began to fidget, their eyes riveted on the wall clock, watching the minute hand creep toward the end of class. A breath of relief came near the end of class when a young artist broke in on the teacher's monologue to talk of creativity in the search for God. The children liked that, but then the bell rang.

The children picked up their things and ran out. Some adults chatted with the artist, while Wah Z collected his coat, shoes, books, backpack, and pens, which were scattered all over the room. The teacher was in a hurry and waited impatiently for Wah Z to quit fumbling with his things and get out.

The religion he tries to teach the children is in pieces and scattered everywhere, just like my things, thought Wah Z.

By the time he got his shoes on, Wah Z was late for Religious Doctrine, his next class in another building across the street. The simple, elegant, old building resembled the U.S. White House but was in a park and sheltered by a grove of trees. Two enormous front doors, like cathedral doors, dwarfed him, but the one on the right swung back easily.

The interior was done in an off-white decor. A sea of students swept in all directions to classrooms that ringed the lobby. On the left, a staircase led up to a low-ceilinged mezzanine level, where more students headed for class. Hallways on the ground floor ran to the right and the left of the main lobby, suggesting classrooms in other wings of this mammoth building.

For a moment, Wah Z studied the organized chaos. A bell sounded, and the last trickle of students melted into these caves of religious education. A straggler hurried into the lobby, and Wah Z stopped him for directions. The student took Wah Z to a wall behind the stairs, pressed an ornament shaped like a golden eagle, and a secret stairway appeared behind a sliding door.

"Plass's class is up there," said the student and rushed off to class.

Wah Z climbed the stairs to a spacious classroom done in the same off-white decor as below. This room was a miniature of the main lobby, with small classrooms spilling from the center hub, which was for Plass's class of advanced students.

This was a seminary: religion classes were thrown at a student for two years before he went into the field as a vicar. How interesting to find religious field missions on the Astral Plane, even as on earth. One wouldn't think it, but many people who die on earth and go to the Astral Plane continue to promote beliefs they held on earth.

Fortunately, it was the first day of a new school term, and the class was still to settle down. Students chatted while Plass scuttled back and forth to a side room for teaching materials. Plass was notorious for scolding latecomers, so Wah Z was relieved that his late entrance had gone unnoticed. He slipped into a seat on the second tier and spread his books, papers, pens, notebooks, and coat on and around his desk. His stomach ached when he thought of enduring two years of this highly structured study of religion.

55

Wah Z could not help but compare this mentalized religion with the clean, simple teachings of ECK, which show that Soul's unfoldment depends upon the Sound and Light of God. So easy, he thought.

When Plass reentered the room, Wah Z was excitedly explaining the simplicity of ECK to classmates seated near him. "I'm going to tell Plass about ECK," he said. Their faces turned white; Plass might shout down heresy.

Stuffing books and supplies back into his backpack, Wah Z went down to talk with Professor Plass at the side of the room. The other students paid them little mind.

"All this study of religion has nothing to do with God, only with the mind," said Wah Z. "The mind can never lead anyone to God."

Plass, sensing a heretic in the classroom, shot a critical glance at Wah Z over the top of his glasses. "Is that so?" he said sharply. "Then what *is* important?"

"Only the Sound and Light of God."

Plass continued to move about, more slowly now, but still arranging charts and notes on his desk. "Has the 'Sound' a sound?" he asked scornfully.

"Many," said Wah Z. "For instance, the twitter of birds."

"Oh, really?"

"Well," said Wah Z, "maybe *twitter* isn't really the most inspiring example, but what about the sound of bells?"

"Bells?" asked Plass, with a blank, comedic, Jack-Benny stare.

"Well," Wah Z conceded, "*ding* is not quite it either—you'd have to hear it."

"Do you have anything else, young man? I must get on with class."

Wah Z was silent, then said, "There *is* the sound of HU; everybody knows HU." And he began to sing the HU.

Touched by this compelling musical note of God, every student in every classroom began to sing HU with him. The sound of HU filled the whole building, on all floors, in every corner. The professor was startled by the rich, vibrant Sound that enveloped every part of him with serenity; he stood quietly, bemused. The sweet music of the HU continued to ebb and flow like a towering ocean wave; its effect was beyond words.

Wah Z stopped singing, and all the others stopped too; the room grew quiet as students returned to their books. Cradling books under his arm that did not fit the backpack, Wah Z started for the door. What need has one in search of God for dead religions of the mind?

But he paused to speak quietly to Plass off to the side. "This religious study you teach is not essential for a truth seeker," Wah Z said.

"Would you then have me stop teaching religious philosophy and dogma?" asked Plass, thinking of his livelihood.

Wah Z furrowed his brow. "No," he replied slowly. "That wouldn't be good either. These students need someone to teach them this knowledge; without it, they'd miss a step and delay their journey home to God."

The fiery, old professor looked quizzically over his glasses. He did not know Wah Z as the Mahanta, but thought he was a disgruntled student making plans to leave the church, so he said, "Are you sure you want to do this rash thing? Remember your Savior."

"Empty doctrines are no food for Soul," said Wah Z softly. "I am free; give me the Song of God, the holy HU. Soul bows beneath the weight of books, but Sound and Light maintain me."

The professor pondered this as Wah Z—agent for the SUGMAD—left the room.

The king wanted the esteem of his people, so he drank a goblet full of the tainted water and became like everyone else.

9

The Illuminated State

The search for truth requires a desire to be free of the human consciousness and a desire for the illuminated state of God Awareness.

Soul came into the world at God's command to cultivate His gardens of living things. But in the beginning, Soul was an immature and selfish being, forever preening Itself in the mirror of vanity. So God decreed that until Soul attained love and overcame the madness of the human consciousness, It could not be a Co-worker in His gardens.

Kahlil Gibran—the Lebanese poet, philosopher, and artist of the early twentieth century—once contrasted the human consciousness with the illuminated state. In "The Wise King" (from *The Madman*), he told of a city ruled by a wise and mighty king. In this city was a well of cool, refreshing water from which all the people drank. Even the king and his court came there for water, because it was the only well in the place.

One night a witch stole into town and poured a strange liquid into the well. "From this hour he who drinks this water shall become mad," she cried, with a diabolical laugh. Indeed, it was as she said. All the people, except for the king and his aide, came for water the next morning and turned quite mad. Throughout the day, people whispered to each other in the market-place, "The king is mad. Our king and his lord chamber-lain have lost their reason. Surely we cannot be ruled by a mad king. We must dethrone him."

The king got wind of the revolt and that evening ordered a goblet full of the tainted water. Both he and his chamberlain drank heartily from the cup, and the people rejoiced because the king and the lord chamber-lain "had regained their reason."

Soul, like these people, was pure before drinking from the poisoned well of human consciousness, but thereafter, It shut Itself off from the holy waters of ECK, the Holy Spirit.

The king could have refused the cup, but he wanted the esteem of his people and thus became mad like them. He sacrificed the illuminated state for a material throne, even as Esau once sold his birthright to his brother Jacob for a coarse meal of bread and a pottage of lentils.

A principal teaching of ECK is that Soul exists be-cause God loves It. The problem is that hardly anyone is fully aware of this, except for the illuminated individ-ual. Set aflame by the holy fire of ECK, his all-consuming love for God gives him spiritual freedom. He demonstrates love through his very being and is ac-cepted into the order of the Vairagi Adepts.

William Blake, the English mystic poet, paid tribute to the illuminated state of love in this little verse:

Love to faults is always blind,
Always is to joy inclin'd,
Lawless, wing'd, and unconfin'd,
And breaks all chains from every mind.

The illumined man pays little mind to others' faults because of the God Light he sees in them. Unbound by all conventions, his heart is free; he dances lightly in the Wind from Heaven.

The Wind from Heaven is the ECK, the Holy Spirit. The wavelengths of all living things are contained within this holy Word of God, which is heard as Sound and seen as Light, and which fills all space. And only those in the illuminated states can see and hear It. This is the food of God, manna from heaven, but how seldom is it tasted in the orthodox churches?

Several years ago, the Catholic church took a stand against religious cults. The Vatican, upset that both Christian and non-Christian groups are winning converts from Catholic churches, made a study to find out why the sects were succeeding. Early conclusions were that some groups use brainwashing, sexual enticements, monetary gifts, or promises of bodily healing to win followers. But the church was looking in the wrong direction. It was not what the other groups offered that cost the church its followers, but what the church itself does not offer.

In any case, no mention was made of ECKANKAR, which offers people the Kingdom of Heaven by way of the Light and Sound.

The Christian church fails in that it no longer teaches the essentials of spirituality—the Sound and Light. People sense this and willingly go to other groups, hoping to satisfy an undefined spiritual hunger.

Why is ECK so different? It brings a complete spiritual turnaround to many, but the good and bad of this depends upon the individual. If he is willing, the ECK renews him, for truth is the sun that illuminates his world; and never again is he the same. Yet those who fear the ECK are better off with old traditions.

The Vairagi Adepts know that the Holy Ghost is not received by baptism with water. In the New Testament, the apostles at Jerusalem learned that Samaria had accepted the new Christian religion. Although the Samarians had been baptized in the name of Jesus, the Holy Spirit still had not come upon them. The apostles finally had to send Peter and John to pray for them, and the Samarians then received the Holy Ghost through the laying on of hands.

In ECK, there is no baptism with water. The individual is linked directly with the Holy Spirit through the rite of initiation. He sings HU, a sacred name of God that brings him closer to the Holy Spirit. The music of the Word is always humming around and in him, but man often does not hear it; his attention is on material things. But whoever hears the holy Word is never far from God.

Soul finally wearies of all those problems that dull Its eyes and ears to God. It now longs to hear the Holy Sound that can lift It to the illumined state of heaven.

Is HU for you? Then you alone must find It.

Written words derive from a place no higher than the Mental Plane, because that is the source of the alphabet, symbols, and thought.

10

What Is Truth?

Pontius Pilate asked Jesus this question almost two thousand years ago, "What is truth?" Whatever the answer, it was sufficient for Pilate to announce to the accusing Jews, "I find no fault in him at all."

Essentially the same question was asked of me by an initiate during the past month. He was disturbed about thoughts that the ECK Masters were only invented by Paul Twitchell in his writings as a cover-up of some sort.

Pilate's question to Jesus will be repeated to the end of time. There is no authority who can give a suitable answer besides the Inner Master. Here is the letter that I wrote to the Initiate:

*   *   *

Your questions about the validity of the ECK teachings are sincere, and I respect your curiosity about the truth of the whole matter. Going back to the fundamental elements of the purpose of life here is something that is second nature to you—earth is a classroom that brings about the spiritual maturity of Soul. When Its education is completed, It must decide for Itself what belongs to the realm of timeless truth and what is merely a subterfuge—a shadow of truth.

To start with, all truth is revealed to anyone who has earned it. Further, one can comprehend only so much of the truth as he has prepared himself for—by one discipline or another. Anything more than his capacity spills over the brim of the mind and washes away.

Usually the seeker is not aware of truth within arm's reach, because his limited vision can capture only the hard realities caught within it. There is nothing wrong with this. There is always another step to truth.

That means no matter how much insight we gain about God, there will always be something that lies beyond the horizon of our understanding. That is simply the nature of truth.

Therefore, we understand what we understand and are puzzled or ignorant about the rest of knowledge, wisdom, and understanding. How can we know what we don't know? This sounds like talking in circles, and it is, because the mind can go only so far before it falls back in upon itself. The home of Soul is populated only with beings of pure spiritual natures; the mind is left behind.

What about any writings that attack the authenticity of ECKANKAR?

Oddly enough, the pattern of the negative worlds requires that truth be pelted from all sides. There must be a foil for every segment of truth on earth, because otherwise it could not exist below the Fifth, or Soul, Plane.

Everything down in the spirito-material worlds requires the balance of its opposite for survival. The enigma of all this is that Soul recognizes the importance of the Negative Power as the educator or teacher, but It strives anyway to rise above restrictions of any kind in spiritual things.

ECKANKAR will always have detractors, since that is part of the educational institution here.

The same was true of Christianity during the first two centuries after Christ. That period saw the development of the static doctrines that today form the Christian doctrines. The fight then was to discredit and control the Gnostics, the mystics who believed that the blessings of the Holy Spirit came from inner revelation.

This stood in opposition to the adherents of the apostolic tradition, clergy who claimed as their authority the figurehead of Saint Peter. As always, might makes right. The fierce battle that occurred then between the inner- and outer-directed forces in infant Christianity is today accepted as the source of the true church. But neither side recognizes that it needs the other for survival.

The point of any saint or teaching is: Can this lead anyone to the Light and Sound of God?

Written words derive from a place no higher than the Mental Plane, because that is the source of the alphabet, symbols, and thought. The Essence of God, the ECK, has at that point just made Its incursion into the realm of negativity from the indescribable worlds of God above.

More information is coming out over time about ECKists who have reported meeting ECK Masters, like Rebazar Tarzs, before they had even heard of ECKANKAR. It is a common thing for people to encounter an ECK Master years before the spiritual leader has even completed his own training for Mastership.

These stories will come out in the ECK teachings over the coming years. But it is interesting to find that those who require proof of the existence of the ECK

Masters are in the same position as the central character found himself in *The Journey to the East* by Hermann Hesse.

Hesse, himself, once met these great beings of the brotherhood he called *The League,* but then lost contact with them. For years he wandered aimlessly about, making fruitless efforts to complete his mission of writing about them without disclosing their secrets.

Finally he did meet them again, and his doubts about their authenticity fell away like a bad dream. They had been around him all the time, going about their missions, not in the least concerned about what his doubts would do to their state of being. They did not need his insecurities and doubts for their survival and well-being.

* * *

Criticism of the path of ECK is a test that will only tax the doubter. The final outcome is that he must come to his own settlement with the Divine ECK.

This is the law of the worlds!

The doctrines which constitute the outer works of
ECKANKAR are revealed in *The Shariyat-Ki-Sugmad*.

11

ECKANKAR, the New-Age Religion

For years we've bent over backward to say in the same breath that we are a spiritual teaching, yet not a religion. ECKANKAR is, in fact, the New-Age Religion. The ECK Itself is not a religion, of course, because It is the Audible Life Stream. But when "ECK" is used in place of ECKANKAR, then we can well call it the new religion of the age.

An issue that many ECK initiates still need to deal with is how ECKANKAR differs from all other religions. It is certainly not an orthodox religion, although it is a religion.

The Shariyat-Ki-Sugmad, Book One, makes an interesting comment about the relationship between mainstream religions and the Godman, the Living ECK Master. The two are not in violent opposition to each other, as mental purists in ECK would like to think.

Says *The Shariyat:* "In the end he [man] will learn that all religions established so far throughout the world have their origin in the Godman, the Living ECK Master who comes to this world, lives among humanity, and guides all footsteps to the Kingdom of God. Every

73

religion in this world is a living testimony to this sacred truth."

There is clearly a close tie between the Godman and the religions of the world. In fact, *The Shariyat* gives the Godman of the times credit for establishing each one of them. He brought forth a new religion from the warm ashes of fading religions, which had lost the original ECK doctrine of Light and Sound. The light of these religions had flickered and gone out, and so they could no longer serve their people.

Thus we must make a distinction between ECKANKAR, the New-Age Religion, and the customary, timeworn religions.

Any religion, and this includes ECKANKAR, has a body of beliefs it holds as truth. These are its doctrines, and these doctrines taken as a whole are called its dogma. Dogma is only a word that is used to refer to the belief system of a group.

The doctrines which constitute the outer works of ECKANKAR are revealed in *The Shariyat-Ki-Sugmad*. Their source is the Sound and Light of ECK, yet they come to us indirectly. The Sound and Light are first stepped down in energy, then they take shape as the holy works of the Shariyat-Ki-Sugmad, which exist in the Temples of Golden Wisdom on every plane of God. By this divine plan of making the teachings of ECK available everywhere, any seeker can find the higher teachings, no matter where he is spiritually.

ECKANKAR alone of all the religions carries the greatest amount of Sound and Light, for its doctrines come straight from the ECK.

Paul Twitchell did not always make it a point to say "orthodox" when he spoke of religions, but that is what he meant. When he speaks of the failure of religion, he is speaking of the failure of *orthodox* religion. Remember what *The Shariyat* spoke of above: The origin of all established religions is in the Godman, the Living ECK Master.

Those who have reached God-Realization do not need any religion, including ECKANKAR. But the path of ECK is a bridge to help mankind unfold from the human state to the God Plane. ECKANKAR is an instrument of God created expressly for the spiritual liberation of mankind, an all-important step in the evolution of Soul.

ECKANKAR is the New-Age Religion. As such, it encompasses a body of principles that are its doctrines. Those who say that there are no doctrines in ECK are wrong. *The Shariyat* speaks of "the doctrine of ECK," not to mention the doctrines of cause and effect, the ECK Marg, and liberation.

Paul Twitchell, in *The Spiritual Notebook,* told how the ECK may appear to mankind: "To some people ECK will appear as spiritualism, to others as some form of cultism, and to still others as a highly complex religious body like the Buddhist or Catholic faiths. ECK takes advantage of whatever opening is available to It, be it a single or collective state of consciousness. Outwardly, ECK makes Its appearance wrapped in the rituals, elegant trapping and utterances of the founders. A closer examination will show, however, that ECK is hidden in the written scriptures and sacred literature of the world's religious bodies."

Notice how Paul simply accepts the fact that the ECK meets the spiritual needs of *all* people. All will get what they need from ECK. The Mahanta always provides Soul a way into higher spiritual states, and so every religion may be a right means for unfoldment, if it can satisfy the needs of the people who follow it.

So we come back to ECKANKAR, the New-Age Religion. We see that its tenets are otherwise known as doctrines, some of which are given above. *Doctrines* simply means any body of knowledge that is taught: There is nothing mysterious about the word. Many spiritual things are taught in ECK, and when we consider Its tenets, principles, or doctrines in their entirety, then they are called the dogma of ECK. This means the body of doctrines that form the outer teachings. For example, the four principles (Precepts) of ECKANKAR are part of its dogma:

"1. There is but one God and ITS reality is the SUGMAD.

2. The Mahanta, the Living ECK Master is the messenger of the SUGMAD in all worlds be they material, psychic, or spiritual.

3. The faithful, those who follow the works of ECK, shall have all the blessings and riches of the heavenly kingdom given unto them.

4. The Shariyat-Ki-Sugmad is the holy book of those who follow ECKANKAR, and there shall be none above it."

These and other statements of principles and beliefs form the doctrines, and collectively the dogma, of ECK.

By and large, orthodox religions are spiritually weak because their clergy must rely upon moral laws and written scriptures for their authority. With ECKANKAR, we find the balance of the mind and heart teachings: the outer and inner. The outer and inner teachings spell the difference between ECK and ordinary creeds. The teachings of ECK shimmer with life because the Godman, the Living ECK Master is both the Outer and Inner Master. He undertakes to show all seekers how to open themselves to the Sound and Light of God. And so ECK is a living path.

76

And yet, a Christian who lives the Law of Righteousness is far superior to a chela who engages in useless arguments with other chelas about whether there is dogma in ECKANKAR. Even though we are ultimately on a path that is centered upon the inner reality of truth, we do need the outer expression of truth while in a human body.

Anyone who truly accepts the inner guidance of the Mahanta will have little trouble understanding him. Such an individual enjoys a rich spiritual life, and he is a lighthouse for others to find their way to God.

One whose faith in ECK is easily shaken by things that have no permanence will never in this lifetime realize the wonderful Teachings of the Heart. He may gamely hang on to ECKANKAR, but he will always be in the background with his bitter tongue, trying in vain to understand what ECK is all about.

Still, there is room for him, too. ECKANKAR, the New-Age Religion, is a path for all.

Just as the sport of judo turns an assault into a protective force, people with a high state of consciousness immediately make a plan to turn negative energy to advantage.

12

Storms of Trial

S o the clouds have broken, and the boiling turbu-
lence has surfaced. This article is a review of the
fundamental areas of spiritual growth you need to know
if you are to go further on this unique path of
ECKANKAR.

ECKANKAR is here to stay. Born in controversy, its
future points to more rocky ground ahead. Its destiny in
seed form is to become a major spiritual teaching during
this life cycle. But this possibility still remains to be
seen.

The future shows more tests and tribulations to
come, and the weakhearted should find another way to
God. The connection between the inner and outer teachings is that Soul is strengthened and emboldened by the
rigors of trials on the physical level that try to shake It
loose from the Tree of Life.

Those of you who wish to follow another path have
my goodwill. The ECK has created as many avenues to
Itself as constellations light up the heavens at night.
Each path is as precious as another, for the Audible Life
Stream makes no distinction in giving Its profound,

impartial love to Soul. ECKANKAR is still held out to be the most direct path to the heavenly worlds of the SUGMAD.

The Living ECK Master is a friend in the hard times. His purpose is not entertainment, but he labors to open the initiate's Tenth Door, the doorway to heaven. He opens the door to each greater step in consciousness, such as the cosmic-consciousness step, the ECKshar step, the Spiritual Realization step, and God Consciousness. The door is opened, but Soul must go through it.

Events to date bring up a good question: Is this the path for me? Maybe it's not. No one will hold you back from the path of your choice. For any member who would leave, I would appreciate your notice of intent to resign from ECKANKAR. You are free to go in peace.

No one is to accept anything about his relationship with God upon another's authority. It must all be on his own. The Mahanta, the Living ECK Master accepts suffering and cares in secret for the spiritual welfare of his beloved ones. But his concern is largely unknown to them.

The trivial things, the social niceties, tie us to the Astral Plane. The Living ECK Master cuts through all the superficial concerns of the God seeker, but the seeker, in ignorance, chides the Master for his slowness in meeting endless desires. The Mahanta waits and watches for a sign of recognition from the chela who finally catches a glimpse of the ECK Light in the face of a fellowman.

A crisis is an opportunity in disguise. A solution is hidden in the folds of every reverse. No matter what is thrown into our face, there is a way to roll with the punch.

People with a high state of consciousness are not frozen into inaction by terror brought about through disasters. They immediately make a plan to turn the negative energy to advantage. At this level of creative imagination, Soul is in a condition of survival. The lesson of the worlds of matter is to develop Soul's ability to ride the crests of life. This is *vairag,* detached love.

A good example of a sport that turns an assault into a protective force is *judo.* An offshoot of the more aggressive form of unarmed combat, *jujitsu,* this sport uses grappling and throwing holds to turn the aggressor's strength against him. Timing and balance let the weaker person overcome the stronger one by using the energy of the attacker and deftly converting it into the art of self-defense.

The Wayshower teaches that kind of survival to his students in spiritual things. His simple methods are usually overlooked as he arranges the chela's karmic debts into some semblance of order. Karma due for repayment is fed back to his charges in accord with the Law of Economy.

The Shariyat-Ki-Sugmad, Book Two gives other titles for the Mahanta, the Living ECK Master, some of which are: "the Godman, the Vi-Guru, the Light Giver, protector of the poor, the king of heaven, savior of mankind, the scourge of evil, and the defender of the faithful. He is the real and only power in all the universes of God."

But this recognition lights only in the eyes of those who love him.

Here is something to know: The initiate is the ideal and standard by which all men are judged. Yaubl Sacabi told Paul Twitchell that the ECK wants Soul's return to the simple and honest—Its original nature.

Compassion, frugality, and humility are Its essence, for they are absent in the worldly man.

Fubbi Quantz, the ECK Adept responsible for the management of the Katsupari Monastery, told Peddar Zaskq (Paul Twitchell) that cleanliness of mind and chastity in body are of importance in the works of ECK. Spiritual strength cannot be separated from the moral qualities of mankind.

The Mahanta never goes out of his way to anger any creed or religious institution, but he draws a sharp line between the ways of Kal and those of SUGMAD. He stands at the head of the Order of Vairagi and bows in humble submission to only the SUGMAD.

The outer teachings in the books and discourses are but a guide to the Inner Master, who opens the Third Eye, which is the Spiritual Eye, to the Light and Sound. When either of these aspects of God come into your awareness, you have been touched by the hand of the Lord.

Storms are yet to rage; the clouds of greater ones lurk on the horizon. Each tempest will try to put an overpowering fear into your heart, in order to scare you onto some detour to God.

A slow but steady building program is under way on all fronts in ECKANKAR. I want to go slowly with each project and build well rather than hurry and build on sand. There will be plenty of work for each of you.

The initiates who stay with ECKANKAR must have courage such as the Spartans displayed against the Persian army in 480 B.C. Xerxes, the Persian king, returned to Greece a decade after the Athenians had soundly defeated his father, Darius. Xerxes' plan was to punish the Greek cities for that outrage to Persia's national pride.

The defense of the passes into Greece fell to only three hundred Spartan soldiers under the command of Leonidas, king of Sparta, an ally of the Athenians. This small band of defenders stopped the full Persian army and bought time for the Athenian navy to sail into a strategic position in preparation for its own encounter with the Persian naval forces.

The three hundred Spartans withstood the Persian army for several days until a traitor showed the enemy a poorly guarded goat trail. Although betrayed, the Spartans made a heroic stand that is still regarded today as the highest example of courage.

Their valor allowed the Athenian navy to win a resounding victory over the invading Persian fleet. For the short time that the Greeks could put aside petty jealousies and work in unity, they enjoyed freedom from Persian rule. The same kind of courage will be required of initiates during the years of rebuilding we face.

The future of ECKANKAR will continue to follow a tumultuous course. The rage of the Kal forces was present at its birth in 1965 and will follow it through its youthful development.

But Soul, a particle of God, is blessed with the gift of creative imagination, which finds a solution for every problem.

Ironically, once the colonists had the right to practice their own styles of Protestant religion, they took up the tools of persecution against outside groups like the Quakers.

13

When Discipline Goes Wrong

A path like ECK has a great responsibility to give freedom to each individual who accepts its precepts. This is said in light of the abuses that have occurred on earth in the past in the name of religion.

The fledgling Christian church saw its early members martyred by the Roman soldiers, because the Christians would not give obedience to the gods of Rome. But when the church itself became a power to be reckoned with in the following centuries, it began to persecute in turn any who did not worship God according to the prevailing beliefs of the church. This led to the infamous Inquisition, a Roman Catholic inquiry into heresy that showed little regard for individual rights.

Of course, a religious group has the right to include members that agree with its doctrines and to exclude heretics. Otherwise the very life-force of the group is destroyed.

A problem occurs, however, when a group becomes so powerful that it goes beyond culling its own flock and begins to send missionaries into a community to persecute those who refuse to join it because they already have their own religion. At this point the more powerful group's internal disciplines have gone wrong.

Paul Twitchell warned about such an abuse of right discipline in *ECKANKAR—The Key to Secret Worlds*. "If a person must be sacrificed to gain something," he said, "it cannot be either moral or good, no matter how much society tells us it is."

Yet this is the common practice, as history blushes to tell. It is one thing for a religion, such as the medieval Roman Catholic church, to excommunicate its heretics, but quite another to torture or kill them. This is not to point a finger of accusation at the Catholic church during its more scandalous periods of history, but to point within the human breast of all ages to say: The spiritual imperfection that allowed mankind to commit violence against individual beliefs in the past is still alive today.

Nobody likes to hear that.

Such a feeling of superiority of one human over another is vanity, one of the five passions of the mind. While people may accept the teachings of their group as best for themselves, they must take care to remain within the discipline of ECK, or Spirit, and realize that these very same teachings may not fill the spiritual needs of people outside their group.

Vanity has its play when the members of a religion carry their beliefs beyond reason and insist that their doctrines are the best for everyone. Vanity is then a short step to anger, another of the five passions, which will not hesitate to use force to make all within reach follow the tenets of the religion. This is a case of the discipline in a group gone wrong.

Colonial America was to be a refuge for minority religious groups to enjoy freedom from European church-controlled countries. Ironically, once the colonists had the right to practice their own styles of Protestant religion, they took up the tools of persecution against outside groups, like the Quakers. When the Quakers arrived in New York, Massachusetts, and Virginia, they found severe laws passed against them. The two latter states finally banished the Quakers, fixing the death penalty for those who dared to return from exile.

We find that the United States of America was established as the nation of religious liberty. But even today, the ideal of our forefathers struggles along as new religious groups, including ECKANKAR, are subject to the age-old tools of oppression. But now the discrimination is in the subtler forms of zoning laws meant to bar us from Christian communities, and heated community meetings controlled by wild-eyed people who enjoy the climate of religious freedom in the United States but want to deny it to others.

They are criminals in spirit like their ancestors— the Roman soldiers who crucified members of the new Christian cult. They are like the monks of the unholy Inquisition. They are no different from the Protestant tyrants of Colonial America who put the death sentence upon Quakers who ventured into the "wrong" communities. This is when a group's discipline has gone wrong.

Back in 1969, a high-school teacher carried out a classroom experiment in Palo Alto, California, that resulted in a chilling study of the ever-present dark side of human nature. This episode was written into a novel called *The Wave,* by Todd Strasser. It was later adapted into a prime-time television drama by ABC, and thousands of good Americans were shocked by it.

This high-school teacher showed his senior-high-school class a film of atrocities committed by the Nazis in the death camps during World War II. The students watched the screen in disbelief and horror as the SS guards forced prisoners to feed huge ovens with thousands of corpses, which were stacked up like firewood. When the film was over, the students wanted to know how it was possible that millions of people could be destroyed in a country and then have 90 percent of the population claim to know nothing about it.

The teacher had no answer, except that the small group of Nazis, only 10 percent of the population, was a highly organized unit and the majority of the people were afraid of them.

It troubled him that the history books gave no reason why the Germans let the Nazis become so powerful. Perhaps more disturbing, the students thought that World War II was ancient history, that such acts of barbarism could not happen today. They thought it was a quirk of history that a whole nation could be caught up in the vanity of thinking they were a superior race. But it was just this sort of vanity that led to the extermination of so many minorities—because the Nazis called them inferior.

As part of a "show, don't tell" experiment, the teacher altered the behavior of his class in just two short weeks. They came to think of themselves as members of a superior group. This group was *The Wave*.

In those two weeks, the students adopted a rigid military bearing, developed a salute to recognize other members of the Wave, and gave their devotion to three mottoes of group unity. So far, this was acceptable behavior, because all groups fashion themselves along similar lines. After all, even a country such as the United States of America has a Constitution and a Bill of Rights, and its people do salute the flag.

But the discipline in the Wave went wrong when its members began to intimidate and beat up students who were not members of their group. Again, we see the abuses of the Roman soldiers, the Catholic Inquisition, and some American colonists.

In ECKANKAR, we stand for religious freedom for every individual. Many of our own ancestors helped tame the North American continent. It is only natural to expect other religious groups, who do not share our beliefs, to grant us the religious freedom to worship God in our own way.

Can both we and our neighbors keep the disciplines of our groups in line?

History teaches of nothing more brutal than when any group's discipline goes wrong and the freedom of an individual is made a scapegoat on the altar of religion.

Will mankind ever outgrow its vanity and hate? The wheel of karma turns again, and we must wait to see.

Paul Twitchell's task was to study all the religions, philosophies, and metaphysical disciplines of the world and compile their elements into an easy-to-understand set of writings.

14

Paul Twitchell: The Writer

Imagine, for a moment, what a colossal venture it must have been for Paul Twitchell to gather up the bits of ECK truth again and put them all together in one set of writings.

It took the talents of a particularly tenacious man who loved words, to cut through the red tape and get the job done.

Can you imagine yourself in his place: The spiritual hierarchy has given you the mandate to study all the religions, philosophies, and metaphysical disciplines of the world that you can get your hands on. That done, you must now compile the elements of them into an easy-to-understand set of writings.

"Your mission," says the hierarchy, "is to put these rare golden teachings into the midst of the prevailing thought among mankind today." Then the ECK Masters of the Vairagi file out of the room in silence and leave you to your own resources.

That is what happened to Paul.

What kind of a man was he, that the ECK Adepts should select him from among their number and give him this seemingly hopeless chore? Many Souls, you will remember, had earned the right to hear of ECK in this lifetime.

Who had suffered as much as the most sorely tested among them, who had cried to God in despair for enlightenment, or who had loved the ways of the SUGMAD with all his being? None other than Paul Twitchell.

Paul was a fierce defender of his privacy. Perhaps this is why the date of his birth is left in such an indefinite state. The most complete data at hand puts his birth in 1908. Future research by historians will no doubt bring out many of the obscure details of his life before Rebazar Tarzs, the Torchbearer of ECKANKAR, passed the Rod of ECK Power to him in 1965.

Paul was the one responsible for an avalanche of press releases about himself that began a few years after he got his first position in the work force. Public officials, he had found, showed an amazing deference for titles and social position. Therefore, Paul thought it a worthwhile project to put down a list of his grand accomplishments and get them into *Who's Who in Kentucky*.

At the tender age of twenty-seven, when most of us (including Paul) have only a morsel of the credentials usually needed to impress an editor of a publication such as *Who's Who*, Paul scratched out a sketchy résumé—sketchy by the standards of even the most charitable of readers—and got it entered into the historical records of his home state.

Armed only with a typewriter and an overripe imagination, Paul slipped his name in among the august dignitaries of Kentucky. Most bore the weight of advanced age, but they could also boast rich personal histories of offices won on the way to fame at the top of their respective professions.

Although Paul's list of credits looks impressive at first glance, a closer scrutiny shows that his skills were few—spanning a mere seven years. During that time he had been the physical-education director at two local colleges, had held a similar post at two small-town YMCAs, and had served as an assistant director of physical education at Ohio State University—the most commanding of his positions. He had furthermore just ended a year-and-a-half stint as the City Recreation Director of Paducah.

As a final touch Paul tossed in this item: "contributor of articles to *Athletic Journal*"—a hometown Paducah publication.

The amusing thing about his *Who's Who* entry is that Paul wrangled a place for himself in the company of renowned physicians, geologists, mining engineers, executives, lawyers, and well-known politicians. He must have enjoyed a good laugh when he found his name actually published among those of the distinguished leaders of Kentucky.

This was the raw beginning of Paul's untiring push to be his own best press agent. Perhaps unknown to him in his youth, there was the need for him to learn to write with clarity and also to be grimly persistent in the promotion of his books and articles. The ideas to come in the future—called ECKANKAR—would run into strong opposition from the world. His mission would demand every ounce of willpower and craft to make it work.

The power of the pen is an all-powerful companion in a culture whose history is passed along to its children through written documents instead of oral legends and myths as were once given from father to son.

As a blooming writer who fully expected to support himself with his writing, he pounded out a flood of poetry, articles, and novels on his typewriter. Doggedly he placed his copy where the eyes of the public might find it.

One such place he sent material was to the popular *Ripley's Believe It or Not* column, which featured Paul on several occasions. The first time he got mentioned in it was quite by accident. A Kentucky farmer had designed a mailbox in the shape of a prehistoric creature. Paul submitted this bit of oddity and was surprised to find that *Ripley's* mistakenly gave him the credit for the peculiar mailbox. For weeks thereafter, people from all parts of western Kentucky dropped by the Twitchell house to see this marvelous creation that had caught the region's fancy for a brief interval.

But Paul quit sending tips to *Ripley's* when he learned that no payment was forthcoming to any contributor of published items.

Fame is but a fleeting thing. The existence of Lemuria and Atlantis is laughable to our reputable historians, even though so little is known about a relatively recent event such as the life of the first American president, George Washington.

In the same vein, Paul remarked that Paul Revere is renowned today only because a good publicist told his story in a catchy way. The publicist? Longfellow, who wrote the poem "Paul Revere's Ride." Another party, William Dawes, Jr., may have even ridden further than Revere, but because fate did not assign a good journalist to him, he is largely ignored in American history.

"This is why so many last throughout all history," Paul observed, "because somebody else made them famous, in poems, etc." He believed that somebody else's publicity had made Freud famous, as well as Caesar Augustus and Jesus of Nazareth.

Ancient records must be found to support things like the lost continents and old-time presidents, for without these records, their history is not taught in school textbooks. They are memories lost in time.

How does all this tie in with the whole picture? A number of good writers will emerge from among the ranks of the initiates in ECK. They will become the master writers who will carry the news of the Divine Spirit to places where people are ready for it. This will augment what is already being done in song, story, art, letter-writing, community work, and other ways limited only by the imagination.

In 1971, Paul gave a directive to build up the name of the Mahanta, the Living ECK Master until it became a household name.

"Please remember," he reminded in a personal letter, "the Mahanta is the state of consciousness, and the Living ECK Master is the physical body for the Mahanta state of consciousness—see the difference?"

Paul said to publicize "that the Mahanta is responsible for world changes—this is the spiritual revolution that ECK is bringing about in this age." The vision of his mission crowded out all minor interests, and the ECK kept giving him a wealth of new ideas about how to take just one more step.

The trail of outrageous tales surrounding this unique character from Paducah, Kentucky, may someday fill volumes, but every action and experience from his youth on was ever drawing him closer to the bosom of the ECK for service in Its cause.

A remarkable writer, this man from Paducah. But he was only the vanguard of the wave of ECK writers who would later follow the trail he blazed as the Mahanta, the Living ECK Master.

Count me in !

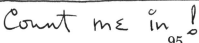

Paul showed the reporter samples of his trademarks, the "Recommended by Paul Twitchell" award, as well as the "Paul Twitchell Sour Grapes Award."

15

"Stop the World,
I Want to Get Off"
...*or* When Will You Leave ECK?

The history of our almost endless incarnations has seen us both embrace, then cast off the Mahanta, the Living ECK Master. The grounds for betrayal seem always so right to our muddled minds. Some behavior of the Master or Mahdis stirs up anger, and a ridge comes up between us and the ECK.

So, folks, stop the world, I want to get off!

Poor little me. Soul in the green state of innocence has a blocked line of vision to the Holy Spirit; It is therefore in ignorance of the object of Its being—to be an envoy for the SUGMAD, but actually, a Co-worker.

"I Shall Not Pass This Way Again" is a telling poem by Eva Rose York about Soul's desire to make the most of Its life on this earth of flowers and winter snows. She dreamed of making each moment count in deeds of service so that the present life is fully accounted for. She caught a flash of Soul finally seeing Its birthright as service to God and not to the ego.

The trouble with most of us in making decisions about spiritual things is that we lack the yardstick of well-rounded experience. Without it, the commands from Soul to the mind get short-circuited, and we are apt to go off half-cocked when the Master does something that is new to our experience. We scurry away in a huff, certain that our desertion will leave a cutting impression of him on others. A trap of the social mind that hurts us more than anyone.

Our judgment is clouded by Kal's sleight of hand. A classic marketing experiment a few years ago shows how easily we can be fooled by false values. The maker of a laundry detergent gave each consumer three boxes of soap powder for use at home. One box was blue, one white, one blue and white. All boxes had the same powder in them. The consumers drew the conclusion that the detergent in the blue box was too weak, the stuff in the white box certainly bleached out the clothes, but the soap in the blue-and-white box was just right for them.

The Master is the overseer of one's karmic burn-off, but the chela sees some of it as good, the greater part of it as crushing. Like the same detergent in boxes with different markings, the chela glosses over the point that the balancing of his karma is a needed operation, and that the good and bad parts are not at odds with each other—they are the same thing.

The Mahanta's plan for Soul's spiritual freedom is not read according to the facts. After reading all the signs of the Master's help wrong, the chela runs off in circles down the track of time, looking for somebody to give him an easy road to heaven. Therefore, the disciple's betrayal of the Master is a historical reality.

Who can know the thoughts of Judas Iscariot when he undertook the betrayal of Christ? Was it greed, anger, or a sting from a sharp word once fallen from Jesus' lips that caused him to do it? Judas risked eternity for thirty pieces of silver, which he used for the purchase of land. But he never got to enjoy the fruits of the land because he fell headlong from a high place, and the fall put an end to him.

The attempt to run away from the Master is a problem as old as time. It happened in the days of old, and a like story is retold still today.

Here comes Paul Twitchell, a social rebel and spiritual giant in a single package. A man who shines with the light of truth is an alien among us, a threat to the dear rules we raise up as a shield to guard us from the hard edge of reality. His personal life and habits were a jolt to people who thought a man of God should be of another order; we like our idols to be without clay feet.

A reporter for a San Francisco newspaper set up an interview with Paul in early 1964. She was to meet him in front of a department store on Union Square, but she had forgotten to ask how to recognize him in the crowd. It was hardly a trick to know that the short man in an overcoat, carrying a bulging briefcase, and wearing a small sports cap on his head was Paul. He darted from one woman to another asking if she were the one waiting for him.

Frankly, he did not look the part of a spiritual man at all. Jesus probably would have moved about the crowd with a measured, dignified walk. But not Paul— he scurried.

Nevertheless, Paul got a lick in about himself, the Cliff Hanger. This person, said Paul, is "the individualist living outside of society, watching what is going on and being amused by it." Men of God are supposed to interfere in the destiny of the human race, not cling to a cliff above it in silent amusement.

Paul dished out samples to her of his trademarks, the "Recommended by Paul Twitchell" award, as well as the "Paul Twitchell Sour Grapes Award." The seal of approval was only a spoof against Duncan Hines and Good Housekeeping for their puffed-up opinion of themselves as the guardians of taste for the American people. He sent his stickers to such notables as Eleanor Roosevelt, to a number of national columnists, and to the creator of the Steve Canyon comic strip. Even the manager of a Shakey's Pizza Parlor got an award after Paul made a visit there, probably to eat a pizza.

The interview splashed some colorful copy into the daily newspaper column, but the reporter's final impression of Paul was less than one of reverence. "Cliff Hanger" sounded like a sport to her, and maybe she was right in her opinion.

A shock to people who feel that high men of God have bodies of physical perfection: Paul's photo in the spread showed him sporting heavy, dark-rimmed glasses. Shouldn't a high man of God know the secret of 20/20 vision?

In a 1970 interview, a reporter left with another view of Paul. She was sure that no one would mistake Paul, with his strong Southern accent, for a spiritual leader of thousands. He looked like a banker, dentist, or merchant. To her wonder, he ordered a lunch of chopped sirloin (well-done), Jell-O, and coffee. A spiritual master who is not a vegetarian must be a charlatan.

Scientologists pelted Paul with letters. The advanced members, the Clears, made an offer to advance him in spiritual matters for a large sum of money. Paul bought none of their sales pitch because they had more problems than did he, an outsider. Although he claimed to have acted as L. Ron Hubbard's press officer for several years in the District of Columbia, he wanted no flak from these people. Paul's tie-in with Scientology during his training as the Godman is another bitter mouthful for some people to chew.

Even in ECK, one's cherished notions about the Master are dashed by the truth of spiritual things. For instance, all ECK Masters do not hold the same high power from the SUGMAD.

Paul wrote to a European initiate about Tamaqui, a Master in Germany during the latter part of the nineteenth century: "He was a minor ECK Master with limited authority to work only that nation—hardly above the station of a Mahdis!"

The inexperienced Soul will snatch at any reason at all to leave ECK, especially when It sees the Master with dust on his feet like everybody else.

The true ECK initiate gets off at the right place— the Soul Plane—when he says to the Mahanta, "Stop the world, I want to get off!"

Will you?

Since the ECK swept over me on a lonesome bridge near midnight in 1970, I have learned the secret of opening the inner channel to let the ECK love come through at will.

16

The Golden Heart

In 1970, I was blessed with the wave of ECK love that changed my life forever. It was the shattering experience of God-Realization.

Of course, I did not know what it was then, and in the years from then until 1981, when I took the Rod of ECK Power, all kinds of fulfillments of the God state came to me by degrees. All these degrees of fulfillment had as their origin the primordial wave of Shabda, Voice of the SUGMAD.

When the Shabda Dhun, the ECK, swept over me on a lonesome bridge near midnight of a cold night in early spring, It was a thundering, crashing wave that was too great for my karma-ridden body to bear. The purification of the Shabda brought me horrible pain, a pain so deep and complete that it is beyond description, for it was both terrible and exquisite at once.

In the years since 1970, I have learned the secret of opening the inner channel to let the ECK love come through at will. No longer is it necessary to wait for the rare occasions when the bruises of life can temporarily soften me so the Voice of God comes through in all Its splendor.

Now It comes when I use the secret method of letting It come to me. It is there for comfort, healing, and joy. In the ability to drink of the pure love of God is the meaning of the term "the God-intoxicated man."

The Golden Heart is "the loving heart," which Paul Twitchell wrote about in *Stranger by the River*. The seeker and the girl were walking slowly along the bank of a river. The seeker looked upon the beauty of God in his beloved and wondered, "Can it be that the search for God is that of two divine Souls together?"

Rebazar Tarzs stepped out from the trees along the river. "Ye know that the greatest of God's qualities is love. For love is the greatest and most sublime force of the universe. Through love the divine qualities of God will shine like the radiant light of the morning sun.

"I will whisper to thee, dear ones, this divine secret," he said. "All things will gravitate to thee if ye will let love enter thine own hearts, without compromise."

Rebazar told the seeker and his beloved that love first inspires the heart as human love. The individual wants to serve his loved ones and his human ideals. By this, "the heart becomes refined by selflessness and love possesses thee."

Paul was rewriting this manuscript in 1957. At the time he was in love with a woman he hoped would be the companion to help him with his life's mission. She was the woman he had met on the inner planes with Rebazar Tarzs, the inspiration for the priceless book of poetic wisdom on love, *Stranger by the River*.

The Golden Heart is full of the love for God and has compassion for those who are lost in the darkness of the human consciousness.

But false teachers abound who say they alone know the real way to God-Realization. These false teachers operate in all the lower worlds. Generally they are theorists who try to give the public guidelines on what the steps to God Consciousness are. But how can anybody tell the way to the SUGMAD unless he has traveled it?

One night the Mahanta, Wah Z, planned to attend somebody else's lecture on the inner planes. The talk was to be about "The Shortcut to the God-Realized State." The lecturer was a red-haired man, broad in the shoulders, and six feet in height. His talk had started twenty-five minutes early because he knew that people seeking truth would be in line early outside the door. If he started ahead of time, the gatekeeper could be instructed to tell people—like the Mahanta, if he should happen by—that the session was in progress and no latecomers would be let in. This way he could skim off easy pickings and not have to bother with someone who knew the living truth.

The lecturer did not want the Mahanta to get in and spoil his little game of deception, but the gatekeeper knew the Mahanta as an old friend, and so the Master entered the lecture room.

The lecturer stopped in midsentence as the Mahanta ambled in. The latter was still thoughtful from a contemplation a few minutes prior to his arrival.

With a strong ring of authority, the redheaded man challenged the Mahanta's tardiness. But the Mahanta felt no need to argue the trivial point that the lecture had started too early and waved him off.

The Mahanta had come to ensure that the teachings of the Golden Heart were given correctly to the people in the audience.

The speaker had the class set up in a strange way. The audience sat in chairs facing one way, and he stood to the side of them, rather than in front.

The Mahanta, the Inner Master, calmly turned his own chair to face the speaker. The man next to the Inner

105

Master did the same, not knowing who sat beside him. As he moved his chair to face the speaker, the man seated next to the Mahanta asked, "What puts you in the calm of the heart center?" The God State of the Mahanta was easy to see, because this man had an open Spiritual Eye.

The whole audience turned their chairs to face the theorist who had it in mind to speak of God Awareness. He was now very uneasy; the people could look him in the eye. He tried to mock the Mahanta again but was waved off.

"Talk," said the Mahanta, "if you've anything to say."

Furious, the man stopped his talk and left because the Living Word, the Mahanta, was too much for a pretender to handle.

The audience had been drawn in to the talk by the glib ads that the speaker had run in the local papers, but when his talk was compared to the Mahanta's presence, it was not even a pale shadow of truth; and all knew it.

Other false teachers who propose to talk of God-Realization set up tests and make a big deal of the signposts of the God State. They say who is near It and who is not. They insist they have made a long study of the matter and are experts in the field, but how can someone speak of God Enlightenment unless he has It?

The closer one gets to the Ocean of Love and Mercy, the more he is the Golden Heart. His love for the SUGMAD outshines any concern for the welfare of his little self.

Paul had an illumination at the age of eight that left him ever after the rebel, the Cliff Hanger. Years of pain and heartache came and went before he had the 1957 experience of God-Realization. Even after that, life crushed and squeezed him until his thinking and emotions were such that he could become the Mahanta, the Living ECK Master in 1965.

The Spiritual Exercises of ECK are the way to the Golden Heart. Once the individual has it, he is never again the same. He has spiritual liberation in this lifetime.

Can a chick reclaim its shell?

17

The Spiritual Crib

"The spiritual crib" is the condition of anyone who judges himself by a yardstick from the past.

One can only receive the gift of God when his heart is pure and gentle, and his mind unfettered by doubts and fears. A question for some initiates arises from the fact that they embraced ECKANKAR when Paul Twitchell was the Living ECK Master. Young on the path of ECK, they had experiences that originated mostly in the lower worlds. This state of self-remembering is important, for it puts one in the center of activity while at the same time he acts as the observer.

Some were fortunate on occasion to work directly with Paul. To awaken the sleeping chela the Living ECK Master may ask a pointed question. In one instance Paul asked a young initiate, "Remember the lifetime we were together before?" She did not. Vainly she tried to recall the ancient setting where she longed to find the ECK Master who could give her the realization of God. Paul's question haunted her for years,

109

serving as a seed of contemplation that led her finally to the liberation of Soul.

When a new Living ECK Master accepted the spiritual mantle in 1971, these early initiates faced a decision. Why were their inner experiences no longer the same with him as they had been when they started with Paul? A reason overlooked was their progressive unfoldment in the years since then.

Some gave devotion to the personality of the Living ECK Master instead of looking to the unchanging Mahanta. Upset and unsettled in their minds with the appearance of a new teacher, it was natural to retreat in thought to their spiritual childhood of several years earlier. To their utter dismay, they found the current revelations far less phenomenal than those of yesterday.

Paul Twitchell stated in *The Flute of God,* "There is first the child who seeks, then becomes the man who looks for God everywhere but in the right place. He finds his teacher, becomes the disciple, and finally becomes the Master himself."

As Soul moves toward the pure God Worlds, the phenomenal experiences fade away and are replaced by the greater Light and Sound of God.

The majority of the ECK initiates cross the bridge from one Living ECK Master to his successor quite easily. They put aside all doubts that arise in their minds. Their hearts remain pure and gentle. Only the dedicated and those who banish doubts, lust, and unhappiness can receive the gift of God.

"When I was led to this path," confesses a recent correspondent, "I was really skeptical ... until I had my first experience on the inner. Now I know that this is and has always been the path for me."

Gradually the dream state changes as we venture deeper into the worlds of our being. Life demands that Soul move either forward or backward. Nothing stands still.

A while ago an ECKist requested special help in recalling his dreams. "Since I received your note a few months ago," he writes, "I have been placing greater attention upon remembering my dreams. Just as you said, the success is really remarkable. Much more than in the past I can recall my dream experiences.... You were quite right, for these dreams are often veiled or hidden from us." His awareness expanded since he opened himself to the guidance of the Audible Life Current, the ECK.

No ECK Master will say to the ECK initiate, "Come, let's put you back in the crib!" Can a chick reclaim its shell? As we unfold spiritually, the reality of our inner life enters new dimensions and we must change with it.

The sincere lover of God endures much testing and reevaluation, but finally he fulfills his destiny and joins the ranks of the Ancient Order of Vairagi. Each of these great ECK Masters once faced the same tests you face today.

A dreamer was shown a future condition through an experience with a crocodile on the Astral Plane.

18

How to Keep a Dream Book

This article is on how to approach your inner experiences and log them in a dream book.

Everyone who sleeps does so because Soul has temporarily left the body. Some modern dream researchers feel that rest is mostly dreamless for the first sixty to ninety minutes, since the brain waves slow down. This "dreamless" interval is said to alternate with a second one of shorter length, which is active dreaming.

In both cases, however, Soul is in Its secret worlds, sorting out events of the previous day, looking for a way to resolve them.

We envy people who not only remember their dreams, but whose dreams contribute new findings to science. These are the researchers who run into a brick wall while trying to solve a complex problem, then get a clue to solving that problem through a dream experience.

A chemist few have heard of was Friedrich Kekule von Stradonitz of Germany. He had a dream which allowed him to make a discovery with widespread commercial use today. In 1865, he spent many hours trying to learn the molecular structure of benzene, a mystery to science. One night he dreamed of a snake biting its tail. From that image came the benzene ring. Benzene is now used in the production of dyes, solvents, and plastics.

Few of us are inventors, but we all have our challenges. Even as Kekule von Stradonitz overcame a snag in his research by means of a dream, we can resolve our problems too.

Rather than disrupting your life through an all-out assault on your dream worlds, in the beginning put just a little attention on them. Instead of trying to record your dreams every day from now until forever, pick one day of the week that is most likely to offer a few minutes rest. You can begin to study dreams during a nap. When you feel tired, set an alarm for twenty minutes, and have a notebook handy. Put your attention upon the Mahanta, the Living ECK Master; but do this in a light, easy way—almost as an afterthought.

Now tell yourself that you will have a peaceful nap and that you will remember a little of what occurs in the other worlds when you awaken. Then go to sleep.

When the alarm rings, jot down whatever you can remember, no matter how foolish it seems. In time, you may expand your study of dreams, because this method is easy to do even in a busy family.

The first rule in keeping a dream book is to write simply. Writing complex ideas in everyday language is hard work. A dream may have so many details in it that you can become sidetracked from the point. To overcome this, write the dream out in full length. Then put it away. At the end of the month, review those inner experiences that stand out. Condense them. Make believe you are an editor on the staff of *Reader's Digest*. Gather the best of your experiences and revelations, if

114

any, and send them to the Master in your initiate report. It is an easy way to resolve karma.

Your dream book is a map. In it, you compile events from your spiritual life. As time passes, a structure will begin to emerge from the special way you record the images in your dreams. You thus become a pathfinder, an explorer, in the heavens of God.

The most mundane help from dreams can be with finances. A dreamer saw a bull. From past dream records, he had determined that the bull was a symbolic reference to the stock market and meant an advancing market. But in this dream he saw the paradoxical image of a bull standing still. He recorded this image with a nice turn of phrase: "It was standing stock-still." He correctly read this as a temporary stall in stock prices, rather than a major decline. Thus he held his position instead of selling at a loss. A few days later, the market advanced again.

A dream book can also give a general warning of danger. An individual may be given an overview of what to watch for, instead of having all the names and faces of wrongdoers filled in. This apparent gap in dream service is no oversight. The Mahanta, the Living ECK Master arranges the dream world of the ECKist. He gives the dreamer enough information to interpret his own dreams, if he will.

Otherwise the dreamer would develop blind trust in dreams and gain little thereby. He is responsible for bringing stability to his own worlds, because he has knowingly or unknowingly let others upset them.

A dreamer was shown a future condition through the following experience on the Astral Plane. Someone tied a chubby, five-foot crocodile to his waist with a long rope. To escape the menace, the dreamer flew into the sky, far above the fields and woodlands. The crocodile

115

followed him like a malignant thing at the end of its umbilical rope. The dreamer supplied the flying power, which gave the reptile a chance to maneuver in its aerial attacks against him.

The dreamer was like the lead plane in a dogfight. Using intricate dodges, he eluded the crocodile's teeth long enough to untie the rope and watch the crocodile plunge to its death.

The dream meant this: Someone in the physical life was going to tie him to a project with a self-destruction device built into it. The dreamer was warned, "Be alert. The plan will backfire." His knowledge of evasive action would allow time to untie the strings that bound him to those with plans to harm his interests. This dream gave him an edge. Taking countermeasures, he prevailed against the conspiracy, which surfaced a few days later.

The following dream is more indirect in its meaning. It tried to show the dreamer the difficulties of descending from a high state of consciousness and going about his everyday life. He found himself on top of a high tower. His job was to climb up and down the tower, a dangerous feat. On one trip to the bottom of the tower, the safety rope around his waist snagged his leg and left him dangling upside down. Desperately, he grabbed at the tower's ladder and was able to right himself and safely reach the ground.

This was a spiritual experience. The elements don't line up as logically as some dream images might. But the dreamer *knew* he was to be careful. He was not to let someone catch him off guard while in a higher state of consciousness. Such a snag could turn his world upside down and possibly destroy him.

Some people simply cannot remember their dreams. When the time is right, however, the Mahanta will help one recall an experience of spiritual worth.

In conclusion, a dream book is a spiritual road map, a record of your travels in the Far Country. Each journey will give you a better understanding of the laws of life. And with it, a fuller understanding of love, for love is the universal doctrine of ECK.

Now is the time to begin your dream book.

"Look forward to each night of sleep, for I will meet you in your dreams."

19

The Sacred Dreamer

The dreamer's inner life begins to straighten out once he takes up the study of ECK. The arena of the dreamer's subtle worlds is graced by the entrance of the Mahanta, who erases karmic burdens through the creative use of dreams.

A common reason for failure in the ECK program is that one accepts inferior spiritual goals. These ambitions include begging the Deity for better health, more wealth, or a loving mate, which are merely desires of the human consciousness. The only profitable object for any Soul is Its return to God. The Living ECK Master introduces the most direct path back to the Ocean of Love and Mercy. In his talks he consistently points to the inner temple, where the Mahanta meets the chela.

The connection between the Inner and Outer Master was indicated by a woman from the Philippines who expressed thanks for a recent response from the Living ECK Master. "Around the time postmarked on your letter," she writes, "I received a similar letter from you in the dream state. I can recall only a few phrases now, but it has given me so much reassurance."

119

The dream experience affords a compatible teaching tool to the ECK discourses. It lets the dreamer sidestep the fear and doubt that often paralyze him during contemplation. With confidence he now greets the Master, who lifts him into higher planes of heaven. Upon initiation, the Vi-Guru establishes an esoteric link between himself and the ECKist. Gently the Living ECK Master removes obstructions of fear, depression, and loneliness. Thus the chela's consciousness opens to receive a measure of Light and Sound.

The fear of death is softened through dreams. An ECKist from the Great Lakes region in the U.S. says: "A couple of nights ago I had a dream ... dealing with the fear of death. I was sitting by a campfire with the Inner Master and asked if Soul survives the body after death. The campfire started to move until it was under me and my body was consumed by the fire. When my body had burned up entirely, I could see that I was still there!"

He learned through his own experience that Soul is eternal and that It has no beginning nor ending.

Fear is confronted numerous times within the dreamer's kingdom. Another individual found herself lost in the basement of a museum. This image represented the imprisonment of Soul in the material worlds. Finally chancing upon the exit, she emerged from the basement into the outdoors. Instantly a tornado loomed on the horizon, but she choked down her terror by singing her secret word. A white light, like ball lightning, then swept toward her, causing even more fright than the tornado. As she continued singing her word, she lost her fear of the white ball of light that now blended in smoothly with her aura. The tornado was forgotten.

Surrender to Spirit conquers fear. An inner experience of the sort that she reported builds stamina to meet other trials in day-to-day living.

The fear motif emerges repeatedly in dreams. A chela from the West Coast of the United States dreamed of an attack by a pack of wolves. She called for help, and in response she heard a "pop." The wolves howled and ran away. Next, the face of Wah Z, the Inner Master, appeared on the screen of her mind, and this touched upon an important realization: Remember to call on the ECK.

And what is the Inner Master? Only the ECK! The Divine Power forms the matrix of a spiritual traveler with whom the dreamer has developed a close rapport.

ECKANKAR seminars help set the inner communication line between Master and chela. At an ECKANKAR Regional Seminar in Greensboro, North Carolina, someone told of having arrived there several hours earlier—but in the dream state. Word had reached him that the Living ECK Master wished to see him. A million and one details cropped up before he could get there. Personal burdens had to be resolved before the meeting. Perplexed, he wondered if the myriad details signified his unworthiness to answer the Master's call. The Mahanta soothed his concern: "Take your time!" After cleaning up the odds and ends, he was ready to meet the Light Giver—first in his dream, and shortly thereafter in the physical.

It is hardly necessary for the Outer Master to shake anyone's hand at seminars. The greater meeting occurs with the Inner Master either during contemplation or in the dream state.

The Dream Master, who is the Inner Master, is empowered to filter profound insight into the dreamer's awareness. The following example tells how an ECKist felt outrage at the suspicion that a Mahdis had recommended he be passed over for initiation. He shared his views of this spiritual injustice with a friend who took the matter into contemplation. An ECK Master came in a dream and handed her a gift-wrapped package. The dreamer started to reject the gift because she felt undeserving of it.

"You already have the gift," he reassured her. "This is only the wrapping so that you will be aware of having received it."

He pointed out that when people try to keep a gift from another, not realizing it is only the empty package that they withhold, they risk losing the gift themselves. Spirit is not fooled. Her friend had actually missed his initiation through a lack of self-discipline. Spirit knows the true facts. Once we surrender our suspicions to the ECK, It resolves the matter for the good of all.

The ECKist now gains command of his ability to move into other worlds, becoming a greater instrument for Spirit. An initiate offered himself for carrying the message of ECK among the uninitiated. He was privileged to introduce a very good friend to ECKANKAR in a dream. His acquaintance was shown the role of karma, as well as what Soul really strives for in this existence.

Two days later his friend was critically injured, but inwardly he had already seen the reason for the karma. The ECKist, on the other hand, found comfort in the fact that Spirit had let him be a carrier of the message of spiritual liberation.

Look forward to each night of sleep, for I will meet you in your dreams. Enjoy the daytime hours when you can try out the ECK principles, for you alone create your worlds.

The Sacred Dreamer treads on holy ground throughout the course of life.

122

Paul Twitchell met her on the inner planes to slowly repair the damage done by the drug to the Emotional and Mental bodies.

20

A Word or Two on Drugs

It is unfortunate when the Living ECK Master receives mail from people on drugs who ask to come into ECKANKAR.

The ECK Masters recognize that drugs, except those lawfully prescribed by a physician, pull the user down to the destructive and degrading level of lust, one of the five passions of the mind spoken of in *The Shariyat-Ki-Sugmad*. That indulgence will, in time, reduce him to the consciousness of an animal.

During the sixties and early seventies, the drug consciousness emerged to where drug users felt compelled to introduce nonusers into the drug scene. It was a popular party ploy to spike someone's food or drink in order to "loosen up" the unwary guest.

Medical researchers were just beginning to focus upon the dangers that drugs caused to the mind. Those were the Pollyannish years when the misuse of drugs increased alarmingly among the nation's youth in schools and the military service. There was hardly any awareness of the consequences being tallied in their karmic records by the awesome Lords of Karma.

It is a serious spiritual violation to alter another's state of consciousness against his will, and this includes introducing drugs to unwilling victims through peer pressure.

The following plea for help reflects the mental anguish caused by a bad first experience with LSD. "The other day," says the writer, "I did something that I really regret so much. I took a hallucinogenic drug. I really don't know why I took it. I suppose it was because I wanted to fit in with the rest of the crowd at school. I had no idea what it would be like. I wish it had never happened. It left some pretty bad effects on me, and I don't know how much longer I can stand it. I feel as if I'm losing my mind." LSD had turned her thoughts to suicide.

If anyone is foolish enough to get sombody else involved with drugs, he must reincarnate with the victim for repeated lifetimes until the effects of the habit are broken. The Mahanta will ignore his pleas to lift him into the higher worlds until the last bit of that debt has been repaid.

Drugs attack and eventually destroy the physical, emotional, and mental fabric of the person who gets trapped by them. One effect noted in business is the user's loss of consistent, rational decisions.

The mind is comprised of four distinct parts. The portion most affected initially by drugs is the Buddhi faculty, the instrument for thought, discrimination, and judgment. An ECKist who shuns drugs generally finds himself more than able to compete heads-on with fellow employees who have succumbed to a treacherous drug habit.

The purpose of ECK is to preserve individuality, which leads to spiritual freedom. The addict opens his

126

aura to lower astral entities and may forfeit the right to follow the path of ECK while under the control of drugs.

One woman related how LSD was put into her drink at a party. The group of people responsible for the prank had decided to bring her out of her shell, thereby drawing her to the point of self-destruction. Intervention by the Mahanta, the Living ECK Master rescued her from the twisted hells of delusion that drove her to the brink of suicide. The ECK quite dramatically prevented her from carrying out that intention. For a number of years after that, the Mahanta met her on the inner planes to slowly repair the damage done to the Emotional and Mental bodies.

The reader would do well to note here the consequences that befell the psychic criminals posing as her friends. Practically all of them have translated in one horrible manner or another. One of the people involved is still alive but has been diagnosed as having a terminal illness. The ECKist, on the other hand, regained her health, thanks to the protection afforded by the Mahanta.

Often when a letter reaches my desk from someone who is mixing ECKANKAR with drugs, I return a letter removing him from the path of ECK until he can rid himself of this destructive tool of the Kal, the negative power.

Little does the drug user know that his suspension is done out of compassion—and regard for the spiritual law of ECK. The outcome for anyone who is playing with drugs while practicing the Spiritual Exercises of ECK is a serious setback in spiritual unfoldment. Let him first drop the habit—insuring that he has gained this elementary self-discipline—then approach the Living ECK Master again to request permission to continue with the ECK works.

The user's experiences with mind-altering drugs, no matter how attractive or fulfilling they might appear, carry him no further than the lower Astral Plane, certainly not to the ultimate objective of God. He does not belong on the path of ECK because of the harm he does both to himself and those around him.

This is a strong warning about the dangers of drugs in the life of a devotee of God. Had I the words, this would be stressed even more strongly. Anyone who disobeys the spiritual law by exposing an innocent victim to the degrading horror of drugs, or uses them himself, must answer directly to the Lords of Karma. The Mahanta, the Living ECK Master leaves him to learn his own lessons.

ECK is the way for the Soul that is sincerely seeking nothing else than the direct path to God. The person must be free of drugs unless prescribed by a licensed medical practitioner.

This is for all to see and know the Living ECK Master's stand on drugs. He merely points out the pitfalls and obstacles that stand between Soul and Its supreme goal of spiritual liberation in this lifetime, and reaching the Kingdom of Heaven.

Visualize yourself walking up to a huge door that guards the entrance into the side of the gigantic mountain of light.

21

Methods of the Black Magician

A man who fails in his duty to God has never fully seen God. In *The Tiger's Fang,* Fubbi Quantz discusses the legend of the fallen angel. It is the story of a being who got high on the ladder of spiritual success but failed in his duty to God.

"Although the spiritual hierarchy might exclude him, God is always willing to help him return to the path again," said Fubbi in a lesson with Paul on the worship of Moloch, the worship of personality. (Read *The Tiger's Fang,* chapter 11.)

The black magician depends upon simple, inexperienced people to promote worship of the personality, for in ignorance is his power. Signs of one in whom the Kal power is stronger than the ECK are several, including: (1) Show him money, and he wonders how to get it from you; (2) make peace in your household, and he will try to break it up; and (3) if you say, "This is Truth," he tries to prove it is not so.

The potential for a fall from grace is a real danger when the lust for power thrusts itself into the foreground. No matter what high station one attains on his journey to God, he can end up a fallen star unless he has truly seen the SUGMAD.

A black magician serves his own pleasure and is ruthless in stripping the unwary clean of all they own, for his god is Mammon. The Light and Sound of God are strangers to his heart, because the passions of the undisciplined self have crept into the deepest corners of what was once the sacred temple of the Most High.

Sorcery came among mankind during Hyperborean times, in the early days of man on earth. The Living ECK Master then was Kai-Kuas, who countered the psychic forces by teaching ECK to the chosen few who could understand him. The Varkas kings ruled with a net of fear woven by the invisible powers of the dark side.

Varkan rulers, versed in the melding of energies for destruction, risked no opposition to their control in the kingdom. Kai-Kuas was discovered in hiding by use of the magic eye, captured, and put to death. However the Rod of ECK Power passed to his successor to thwart Kal Niranjan's attempts to snuff out the divine message of ECK in this prehistoric time.

Kai-Kuas, in the tradition of all Living ECK Masters, went into the Silence. It is understood that all these special agents of God have only a certain allotted time here. Disciples able to see and talk with Kai-Kuas on the inner planes got further instructions from him there. But outwardly, they and others were directed to the next Living ECK Master.

This procedure is the same used by the ECK Masters of all time. The teacher comes to give his message, lifts the more enlightened ones into the spiritual planes, then leaves the earthly theater to work in the Silence, either here or on the other side.

132

Rebazar Tarzs teaches in this manner today, although he still keeps a physical body. He operates in the historical mode that Jesus copied from the Order of the Vairagi.

The ECK Masters stay within their own lineage, working completely opposite the methods of Kal agents, who, through power and fear tactics, struggle fiercely to hold on to every remnant of control.

To countermand black magic, one must depend upon his own integrity. Paul told this story of William Bishop, first curator of an early Hawaiian museum. When Bishop first came to the islands, he got sick to the point of death. Somebody informed him that his mysterious illness came from black magic caused by local kahunas, witch doctors. Bishop broke their spells by simply refusing to acknowledge their power and thus defeated them.

A black magician has a degree of knowledge as to how invisible energies split from the Audible Life Current, but he bends them toward darkness and destruction.

With power to invade dreams, he can bring terror through nightmares. The dreamer quakes, wondering what has suddenly unbalanced the delicate scale of his affairs. Monsters appear, forces tear at the Astral body, and strange, awful phenomena confront him.

Fear grows, and with it, the disarming influence of the magician steals over the victim. In the initial phase he scatters the individual's serenity so as to control the mind. Craving raw power, the magician cares not a whit for Soul's freedom.

A trick used to breach a victim's psychic home is done through a dream where the victim is told to expect a letter from the magician. When he opens the envelope, a posthypnotic suggestion is triggered that enforces the black magician's original dream contact. The individual is duped and unknowingly gives up a little corner of himself to an outside force that is not at all concerned about his welfare.

The black magician creeps into his prey's life, step-by-step. Every emotional trick is used to bind the two ever more closely together.

To survive a psychic attack may take several approaches: (1) A conscious closing of the emotional door against the intruder. Any photos, as well as memorabilia, of a disruptive personality must be put out of the house. (2) The constant chanting of HU or the initiate's personal word. (3) An actual fight on the inner planes whereby the trespasser is driven off by martial arts or some weapon at hand. (4) Getting plenty of rest each night.

The old law of protection is this: "Nothing can hurt us unless we ourselves allow it!"

People under psychic attack must make a decision whether to follow the Lord of Light and Sound, or the lord of darkness. Hesitation creates a split current of energy within one. I've had reports of people who suffered heart attacks because they let their emotions pull them in two different directions at the same time. Forgo the worship of Moloch. The price is too dear.

This technique will bar a black magician from your worlds: Shut your eyes at bedtime and see yourself standing before a gigantic mountain of light from whence flows the most enchanting melody of the Audible Life Stream.

Now visualize yourself walking up the sidewalk to a huge door that guards an entrance into the side of the mountain. The door's mighty construction can withstand a thermonuclear blast.

Enter and pull the door shut behind you. Notice how easily it swings, despite its great height and massive construction. With the door shut and you safely inside the shelter, lock the door securely. Snap the padlock, set the dead bolt, drop the bar into place—then turn around and walk directly into the worlds of Light and Sound.

In extreme cases it is perfectly all right to create several outer chambers inside the entrance. Each chamber is likewise protected by an enormous door; all are secured against the night.

Be aware of one thing: The door of protection is made from the substance of ECK Itself. Nothing can get through It!

The Living ECK Master can help you combat the dark force by use of the mighty Sword of the SUGMAD—but only if you listen.

The connective link with the Mahanta—the globe of light—was simply overlooked by the man because it was such a part of him.

22

The Mahanta and Soul Travel

The mission of ECKANKAR is to show an individual the way home to God through Soul Travel techniques.

An individual's first meeting with the Mahanta, the Living ECK Master can be quite an ordinary occasion, one that excites little interest in God. It may pass without the seeker seeing any significance in it at all. The special moment is lost due to the humdrum conditions under which it takes place.

On the other hand, it may have the opposite effect, causing a sharp reaction in the person who is being approached for the first time by the Master.

For example, a woman from a Sunbelt state of the U.S. tells of the time she met Wah Z in a San Francisco hotel lobby in the mid-1950s. He handed her a copy of *ECKANKAR — The Key to Secret Worlds* by Paul Twitchell, a book which did not suit her tastes. Some of it supported her own philosophy, but overall, it was of no value to her. The visitor kept his identity from her, and all memory of this event was blotted from her conscious mind.

Thirty years later, she learned his name when she went to an ECKANKAR meeting, where she was startled to see his picture on a book jacket; it was Wah Z, the current Living ECK Master. In addition, there was also a copy of *ECKANKAR — The Key to Secret Worlds,* which was not actually published until 1969. Both the man and the book looked the same as she remembered them from the lobby in San Francisco back in the mid-1950s. All the lost memories of that meeting with the Spiritual Traveler came rushing in on her. In the intervening years, she had finished the preparation needed to recognize the Master.

How does her story fit in with Soul Travel? The individual is readied to meet the Master by the trials of everyday life, and after that he begins his training for Soul Travel. The Master can deliver Soul from spiritual darkness, and she had found him.

Soul Travel is a means for Soul to go directly home to God, yet it is surprising to see the many lesser motives that some people have who want to learn it. Some want to be Soul Travelers for healing. Others want it to make a living, to spy on private individuals or steal business secrets, or to get recognition in the news media as solvers of crimes or finders of lost persons. Every motive is given except a real desire for God.

After one meets the Mahanta, the Master uses the dream state to prepare the chela for receiving the Light or the Sound.

An initiate who tried to get to a certain plane in contemplation was taken into the inner worlds by the Inner Master. The Master drove him through a residential neighborhood at night. The houses rolled by quickly. Suddenly, the brightest light one could imagine burst from an empty lot between the houses. Its blinding flash was like magnesium burning in a chemistry class. But the Mahanta, knowing that the pure Light of God would have destroyed the chela due to the impurities in him, sped him past the Light so It would not burn the initiate's sensitive Spiritual Eye.

At first, this individual had heard only the Sound of the plane, which had lifted him to the Far Country. But he knew that both Light *and* Sound are necessary for a spiritual consummation. The Sound got him to this plane, but the Light was to let him see his way through the darkness.

Soul Travel is the process of Soul going home to God, a simple and direct explanation for a public that is unfamiliar with the term; it is the return of Soul to the place of Its creation.

Oddly, even those people who have had an experience of God later forget the close bond that once existed between Soul and the SUGMAD. Some are concerned about the degree of their Master's spiritual station, in comparison with the stature of past Masters.

A quirk of human nature is that it likes to associate with things of distinction, even though nothing was done to deserve it. On Johnny Carson's "Tonight Show" several years ago, Carson named a city on the eastern seaboard, and applause broke out from the audience, evidently from people who lived in that city. With a puzzled look, Carson asked, "What did you ever do for it?"

The people who applauded their city had transferred its fame to themselves, making them feel more important. To them, they were greater individuals because their hometown was a well-known location.

People in religions get a vicarious satisfaction when outsiders think highly of their leader; they feel better about themselves. But this is the social consciousness in man, which has nothing in common with truth.

139

Therefore, would it matter if the leader of ECKANKAR, the Soul Travel movement, were a minor ECK Master with limited authority, as was Tamaqui of Germany in the late 1800s? Would one be more diligent in contemplation if a fully embodied Mahanta walked the earth?

The ECK teachings are intentionally vague about the length of time between the appearances of the Mahanta, the Living ECK Master. The number of years given may be five years to one thousand years, two hundred to five hundred years, five hundred to one thousand years, or several hundred years. Qualifiers, such as "more or less," keep the actual return of the embodied Mahanta an open question.

The Mahanta may return as soon as two years in times of spiritual peril, or the universes may not see him for two thousand years. If it were otherwise, the ECK doctrines would be at the mercy of an outer authority instead of relying upon the inner revelations, which are given to one by the Mahanta, the Living ECK Master.

No Master can take the full title of the Mahanta, the Living ECK Master into the inner planes when he translates from the body. The word *Living* precludes that possibility, for it means a Master in the physical body. Therefore Paul Twitchell is not the Mahanta, the Living ECK Master, nor is any departed Master capable of being put into that category. One who has earned the Mahantaship keeps that state of consciousness when he goes permanently into the higher worlds. Examples are: Lai Tsi, Tomo Geshig, Gopal Das, and others. The expansion of consciousness is a continual process that never ends and goes beyond even the Mahanta state.

Anyone who wonders what to do about a spiritual exercise that tells him to put the image of the Mahanta, the Living ECK Master upon the screen of his mind, should look at the screen and see his spiritual guide. The Mahanta is the ECK, and all who are prepared will meet the Sat Guru. The ECK reaches people through Its living embodiment, the Master of the times, for there is no other way into the Kingdom of God.

There are four main divisions in the line of ECK Masters: (1) the Mahanta, the Living ECK Master, who ushers in a new spiritual age about every five years to one thousand years; (2) the Mahanta Maharai, who is the Living ECK Master working in the Mahanta Consciousness; (3) the Maharaji, the Living ECK Master who is not yet the Mahanta; and (4) an ECK Master, one of the countless, and generally unknown, spiritual Adepts who help the spiritual leader of ECKANKAR in his mission.

Many degrees of power are allotted to the beings in each division, depending upon whether or not they hold the Rod of ECK Power or wear the spiritual mantle of the Mahanta.

The question arises: How can a Fourth Initiate gauge the spiritual level of a Sixth? Does a Mahdis judge the merits of a Maharaji?

Therefore, what matters more is something closer to home: How am I doing with the Light and Sound of ECK? One must be at peace with the idea of a Living ECK Master if he expects to Soul Travel, because the Master is the means given by the Divine ECK for reaching the realms of God.

A concerned Mahdis wrote that he had not had a secret word since his Second Initiation. Nor did he have inner talks with the Mahanta, or any Soul Travel experiences. Was something the matter with the ECK program? He went on to say that he regularly saw a globe

141

of light during the spiritual exercises or later in bed during the dream state.

The connective link with the Mahanta—the globe of light—was simply overlooked by him because it was such a part of him. Anyone who sees the Light or hears the Sound of God is out of the body, even though the eyes remain open. This is one kind of Soul Travel.

The movement of Soul beyond the human senses is such a natural process that one is likely to overlook it in its simplicity. Rather than get discouraged, one should review the nature of Soul Travel in *The Shariyat-Ki-Sugmad* and the ECK discourses.

The anchor points for spiritual growth are in place once one has heard the thin, biting call of Soul and has met the Master. The karmic patterns of the past work off swiftly now, and the chela begins to experience the ecstatic states of spiritual freedom.

Therefore, Soul Travel today depends upon the Mahanta, the Living ECK Master. Everything possible is being done to help Soul reach liberation in this lifetime via Soul Travel, the expansion of consciousness.

Any chela can write to the Living ECK Master in regard to Soul Travel progress, or lack of it, in his monthly initiate report.

When the ECKist awoke, the meaning of the photo-graph in his dream was clear: He was giving light to the two individuals.

23

Soul Travel Today

The old misunderstanding about Soul Travel still remains: that it is an occult projection out of the body, into the Astral Plane. Soul Travel is all-inclusive, however. It is a modern way to speak of Soul on Its journey home to God.

Several phases one may experience while in ECK are these: vision, dream, Soul Travel, ECKshar consciousness, and God Consciousness. Each of these facets is distinguished by an increase in Light and Sound for the individual.

Each stage has a unique order of experience, and each leads to a higher phase. The vision is a pre–Soul Travel experience. The individual is still bound to the physical body and is unwilling to admit to a new search for God, especially if it means venturing outside the security of his narrow human consciousness. But a vision is a good beginning toward reaching the Kingdom of God, or God-Realization, in this lifetime.

An example of a vision is this report from a doctor in California. In contemplation, he relaxed and declared himself a channel for the Mahanta *(pause),* the

SUGMAD *(pause)*, and Sat Nam *(pause)*. After a short wait, he was about to give up, as nothing seemed to happen. Then, via his Spiritual Eye, he saw different colored rays coming down from heaven into him. The different colors were for the Mahanta, the SUGMAD, and for Sat Nam.

Then a voice said to him, "That's not all there is." He got the impression that the rest was the ECK, the Holy Spirit of God. Now he declared himself a vehicle for the ECK, and the whole heavens filled with the ECK, as Light and Sound. "A wonderful experience," in his words.

If one has a vision like this, he is on the brink of seeing the deeper things of ECK.

The dream is commonly the next phase that the Mahanta, the Living ECK Master uses to instruct a new chela. The individual will find his dreams beginning to change texture from his pre-ECK days. The vague cloudiness, the pointlessness, of dreams begins to melt away. One finds a new direction taking place in his inner worlds; it is first noticed as dreams of increasing clarity and meaning.

The illuminated dream is thus the second part of the Mahanta's teaching. Understand, there are no fixed borders between the various phases of experience. Even an advanced ECK initiate may have ordinary dreams and visions, although this is rare. Usually, the higher one goes toward God, the more he actually lives and moves in full consciousness in all the worlds he enters. Dreams and visions are a heightened level of consciousness in comparison to what most people outside of ECK know, but in ECK, our goal is total awareness.

This example of a dream shows the two-part play of ECK: giving and receiving. In a dream, the Mahanta handed the ECK dreamer a photograph of the dreamer and two young men. They were standing next to a lamp-post, and the dreamer was giving them something. When the ECKist awoke, the meaning of the dream was clear: He was giving light to these two individuals.

But this dream led to another experience. In an effort to understand the dream further, he went into contemplation and again fell asleep. Now he awoke to find himself in Sat Lok, the Soul Plane. This was no dream, but an actual visit to this first of the true spiritual worlds. Here he met Rebazar Tarzs, who taught him the way of spiritual maturity. The individual had enough understanding of ECK to teach others. The message was for him to get involved in life.

This was a dream experience that ended in a visit to the Soul Plane, which is the dividing line between the material and spiritual worlds. Notice how there is no hard line of demarcation here between the dream phase and a higher one.

After the vision and dream comes Soul Travel. This is all-important in one's spiritual unfoldment. It means he is making the effort to consciously go into the invisible worlds of God. This is in keeping with the aim of Soul, which is to work for the SUGMAD, for God, in ever-greater awareness.

Although Soul Travel belongs to the lower worlds of space and time, it is often how one passes through the material worlds to the spiritual ones in the most direct way. Therefore, it is a valuable skill that can be learned by almost anyone who is willing to invest the time and patience. Soul Travel is a bridge over the gulf that divides the human from the spiritual consciousness.

Soul Travel is a natural progression that is reached through the Spiritual Exercises of ECK. A chela in Africa lay down in bed, covered his ears with pillows, and listened to the ECK Sound, which was like a sibilant, rushing wind in the distance—but still very close and within him. Soon, he felt a sucking motion at the top of his head, but he was not afraid. He then felt himself totally withdraw from his physical body and hover in space over the bed.

"The whole of this space was lighted with shimmering atoms and bright giant and small stars," he said. He looked at himself and discovered he was in the radiant Soul body, very youthful and full of energy and power.

Then he sang "SUGMAD" in a gentle lullaby. In that moment he realized that all the atoms and all the stars were part of him. As he sang quietly to himself, an energy vibrated continuously and flowed out from him to sustain all things and beings in this unending universe of stars. He felt mercy and love for all beings in this universe of light. He experienced a great Sound flowing from his center, touching and giving joyful bliss, life, and power to all in his universe. This left him in spiritual ecstasy, because of the act of giving.

The ecstasy returns to him even now in his physical state. This was an experience of brief homage paid to the SUGMAD (God), and it has enhanced his life in every way.

This experience began as Soul Travel, but it went beyond that and ended as a spiritual journey to God. A touch of God is not the SUGMAD in ITS fullness, because the God experience, all at once, would devastate the individual, causing a setback for many ages.

The classic Soul Travel experience is leaving the human body in full awareness and having the Light and Sound of God flow directly into the Soul body. But some people have done that in earlier incarnations and have no desire to go through the ABC's of spiritual school again. The Mahanta may give them a few brief refresher Soul Travel experiences, and from then on they

That's me

148

go on to Seeing, Knowing, and Being. This phase of experience in ECK is the ECKshar consciousness. To see, know, and be are the qualities of Soul that are at the forefront of attention in the Soul Plane and above.

Beginners in Soul Travel usually stay close to the body. The Mahanta or his designee will help the individual get above the human state of consciousness and take a short journey in the near Astral Plane. These experiences may include the awareness of moving out of the body, going through ceilings or walls, and flying into a blackness. A patch of light glimmers at the edge of the blackness, and the novice Soul Traveler emerges into the light, which is a world of light.

Here he may walk city streets that closely resemble those on earth. The people, however, are busy with duties that are unknown on earth: welcoming new arrivals who have died on the Physical Plane and are ready to resume their lives on the Astral, guiding people who have come to the Astral Plane by chance during a dream, and serving the spiritual hierarchy in many other things that are routinely done to make life go on in the worlds of God.

Soul Travel is a means of hearing the Sound and seeing the Light of God, in a way which cannot be done in the human body. The Sound and Light are the wave upon which Soul rides back into the Kingdom of Heaven; they are the twin aspects of ECK. When an individual has gone through the phases of visions, dreams, Soul Travel, and the ECKshar consciousness, and is an experienced traveler in all the regions of God, then he receives the enlightenment of God. This is God Consciousness, and nothing more can be said about it here because words fail.

Experience is everything in ECK. An individual can read all the books on faith and spirituality in the library, but reading will net him nothing in the worlds of God. Only experience can take us through the detours and dead ends of life and bring us to the realm of the All. A milestone in Soul's supreme journey to God is the art and science of Soul Travel.

An Akashic reading studies past lives that Soul has spent in the Physical and Astral planes.

24

Way of the ECK-Vidya

Many letters each month request ECK-Vidya readings. The term *ECK-Vidya* actually means total knowledge and is the ability to gain spiritual insight into the most minute part of one's life.

Paul Twitchell estimated at one point that roughly 30 percent of the mail he received requested some sort of a reading. There is a natural curiosity to know about the past, present, and future. At this time, however, only the ECK Masters are able to give these ECK-Vidya readings.

For background, an Akashic reading studies past lives that Soul has spent in the Physical and Astral planes. The next category of reading is the Soul reading, which involves a study of lives spent on the inner planes beyond the physical and astral. The third kind is the ECK-Vidya reading, and it, in addition, scrutinizes the possibilities contained in the future.

Paul Twitchell's spiritual duties became such that he finally discontinued all readings at the end of 1969. It often took him three days to a week in order to complete a single reading comprised of five or more single-spaced, typewritten pages. That service was possible before the ECK membership escalated to thousands of chelas, but became entirely impractical as increasing numbers of people flocked to the path of ECKANKAR in the early seventies and later.

 The ECK-Vidya, remember, is only one aspect of the broad path of ECK to God. One must not allow himself to be sidetracked from his goal of God-Realization.

Should one decide to investigate the ECK-Vidya for himself, it is especially important to research only his own records. It is a violation of the spiritual law to read the personal records of anyone without express, written permission from the Living ECK Master. Only he can determine if an individual has passed all the requirements to be an ECK-Vidya reader. Failure to separate the fields of energy results in a distorted and inaccurate picture, and one does great spiritual harm to himself by reading another's records. As a general rule, the ECK Masters Fubbi Quantz and Yaubl Sacabi no longer scan these records, nor does Rebazar Tarzs.

I did for a while during the course of my training, but never for another individual. This was a personal study under the direction of the Inner Master, the Mahanta. It is found that Spirit provides all that is needed for love and happiness right from the fabric of this present moment.

Only rarely do I bother with the effort of discerning future events, and then only for urgent reasons that cannot be met in other ways.

The questions most often asked concern spiritual matters, finances, health, and family. A chela wants accelerated spiritual unfoldment because of impatience; there is a curiosity about personality strengths or defects; somebody asks for an insight into the dangers of following two paths at the same time, or about the outcome of a romantic relationship.

The Spiritual Exercises of ECK open one to the ECK-Vidya at the discretion of the Inner Master. This is the best approach, for it results in less wear and tear on the spiritual seeker as he enters into the mysteries of Divine Spirit at a pace that is right for him.

One chela reports that he foresaw his promotion and increase in salary. "Funny, I actually saw this event several weeks ago on the inner," he wrote. "Yet when my boss told me, I was as surprised as a school kid getting my first 'A' in school. Seeing events on the inner, and at the same time realizing that I cannot take these events for granted, is and has been a miracle in my life."

The main purpose of the ECK-Vidya is for one to gain a fuller understanding of his own life.

Frankly, most questions that you have can be answered much more simply and to your complete satisfaction by relying on common sense. The remaining, unanswered questions can be researched in the ECK books and discourses, the results then taken into contemplation for a definitive answer. If one is honest with himself, the solution of what to do with a particularly vexing situation soon becomes apparent by using this approach.

Furthermore, impatience and not taking the spiritual works of ECK at a moderate pace can open one to insights he is not ready to see. A young lady wanted to learn the secret way of the ECK-Vidya. She followed a series of spiritual exercises to the letter, and the records opened up for her in the dream state. The results, however, were not what she had expected. The past life that she glimpsed had ended on a tragic note, but it did reveal a weakness in her emotional makeup. This insight let her adjust her attitude so that the emotions held less sway over her than before.

With the conclusion of that experience, she requested that the revelations be stopped, and they were. She now recognized the wisdom of proceeding at a natural pace in her spiritual affairs.

Recently a woman broke the spiritual law by giving so-called ECK-Vidya readings and charging for them. She did a disservice to her clients, misleading them into believing that these readings from the lower Astral Plane were the real thing. In cases like this, one's spiritual unfoldment is automatically halted.

A study of the past is merely scanning dead images. No spiritual student wants that for himself. Rather, one sees and knows the forces and currents that are always swirling around him, for this is the spiritual reality that one seeks—not that of the past, nor the future. This is the meaning of living in the here and now of Spirit.

Anyone can make a thorough personal study of the methods employed by the ECK Masters in order to see his personal Soul records. He must be willing to undergo lengthy disciplines as he is slowly opened up by the Mahanta. As with the study of ECKANKAR, one must be bold and courageous—for the timid never find God.

Our concept of heaven is a starry-eyed fantasy with its jeweled cities of light and angels flitting about like butterflies in a garden.

25

The Soft Kiss of God

Several years ago I got to visit Paris for the first time. Here was the fabled city where the Roman conquerors had set up a colony at a busy crossroads in 52 B.C. Capital city of the Franks in the sixth century, center of the French Revolution in the eighteenth century, captive of the Nazis in World War II, Paris remained the glamorous belle of Europe.

In the airport a woman in her sixties told me with considerable pride, no doubt drawing upon rich memories from the Second World War: "No single man is safe in Paris, and I ought to know—this is my town!"

Paris had been my town, too, on several different occasions in recent incarnations. The last time was during Napoleon's ill-fated march on Moscow in 1812. He had marshaled six hundred thousand troops and crossed the Russian border in June, but by October the Russians had forced his retreat into the biting cold. Only fifty thousand French soldiers escaped the Russian regulars.

Along with other young men from France, I had been compelled to leave my wife and home for war. No choice was given in the decision, for all able men got orders to join Napoleon's forces. The march into Russia was in the summertime, but we hardly ever saw the enemy—a phantom force that always slipped away before a face-to-face encounter in battle.

In late autumn, I fell gravely ill outside Moscow during the hasty retreat of the French. Here my last days were attended to by a young Russian woman whose family used folk remedies to try to restore me from a bout with pneumonia. All attempts were in vain as frostbite further imperiled my waning health.

Napoleon had neglected the needed plans for supplying his large army with food and clothing, and consequently I left that life a thoroughly disillusioned man. His shortsighted plans, plus our run of bad luck, were the reasons for my untimely passing. Our summer uniforms, in rags after the harsh summer campaign, were wholly unsuited as a buffer in the hostile Russian climate.

I brought two strong feelings into this life that stem directly from that period in the early nineteenth century. One of these is a bitter distaste for cold weather, unless it is absolutely necessary; in addition, I respect people who make careful plans for vast projects.

What has this past-life story to do with the spiritual life in ECK? Most people do not know of Soul's ability to be reborn into a succession of lives on earth. Still fewer know how to recall past-life memories so that the lessons from long ago can be put to good use today.

We run our lives as if this stay were it—the beginning and ending of all that's worth reflection. Is it wrong to say that Soul inhabits a physical body but once? That It never before chafed under a master's discipline; that It never left other incarnations at the death of those bodies, to be reborn today for Its further education?

Paul Twitchell raised the curtain on ECKANKAR in the mid-sixties and was the Light Giver until his death in the autumn of 1971. His crowning jewel to quench man's inner longing for God was to put into plain words the knowledge of God's Light and Sound, for without them the gateway to heaven is barred.

The approach to ECKANKAR, the Ancient Science of Soul Travel, is most simple. Its spiritual exercises take us beyond heartache, distress, and disappointment. Karma—the sin of bygone days—is washed clean by the cosmic Light and Sound of Divine Spirit, the ECK, which is the only way to be cleansed of old offenses.

The works of ECK are a tool for whoever wants to make a meaningful study of his mind and emotions. Our character is made up of skills and shortcomings, which have developed in past lives. A reason underlies every twist of personality, and a trauma from a forgotten life compels conduct in a certain way, unless the force of Divine Spirit can enter the consciousness to override the mechanical habits of the mind's knee-jerk reaction to irritations.

Freud and his disciples do not go far enough to help us know ourselves. Mind studies skim the most superficial parts of our character, but they do not ever approach the threshold of the illuminated consciousness of the ECKshar.

Science is baffled when it senses the real inner man, whose profound perceptions evade the superficial tinkerings of behavioral research. Hypnosis, often a frivolous pastime, is the bottommost point that mind healers reach in their search for the unknown being that you are, with your inborn riddles from days of old.

Knowledge of the dead past, in itself, is of little use to us. What good is knowledge without the light of understanding?

161

The visit to Paris brought yet another insight: Creation is finished here. Several years earlier I had seen this visit in a dream which showed the stopover in remarkable detail. The dream was on the mark, right down to the wallpaper in the hotel room. The small, high-ceilinged room was furnished in the decor that was in vogue in Napoleon's day.

Heaven, like Paris, is seen differently by each person who goes there. My impressions about Paris before arrival would have been more flighty, had it not been for the dream that outlined what things to expect there.

Our concept of heaven is likewise a starry-eyed fantasy. Soul Travel is a personal way to see heaven here and now. Once we see it, then we arrange our lives to better advantage both now and in eternity.

We want heaven to be jeweled cities of light (and there are such), with angels flitting about like butterflies in a garden (there are those things, too), but we yearn to tramp the hallowed heights in the company of saints, engaging them in sober debates that run into the ages. What a dull, empty, dreary, and dreadfully useless heaven!

Mercy and grace alone take no one to God Consciousness. That is a hoax by religious thinkers, and it has misled countless laymen in the mainstream religions.

Soul Travel is a spiritual journey that outpaces the universal mind kingdom. It delivers Soul to the Soul Plane, where we enter into the initial stage of self-knowledge.

* * *

An experience in heaven may be quite a common-place thing. For example, a woman and her daughter once approached me on the inner planes for a chat. We had met at an ECK seminar in Seattle, Washington, years before I became the Living ECK Master.

Our stroll took us to their home, where her husband asked for help in moving a chest of drawers from the sidewalk into a bedroom. He held out an apple and several strawberries in payment.

After the chest had been lugged indoors, amid a lot of straining and pulling, he said, in more than jest, "You owe me two cents change." He felt that the fruit was worth more than my help, now that the dresser was inside the house.

Instead of two pennies, I held out two crisp dollar bills. He snatched them away with a mild protest: "I was only joking, but OK."

Sadly I left him, for my help had come from the heart; the dirty feet of greed had abused a gift of love. In doing so, he had incurred a debt with Spirit.

This took place on the Astral Plane, a minor division of heaven. Many people go there when they die, yet the state of virtue among beings there remains woefully low. Negative traits follow us from earth to heaven, then back to earth again in later lifetimes. Karma and reincarnation are ruthless predators, and no one can escape them unless his strong thirst for freedom brings him to the Spiritual Traveler, the Living ECK Master.

The man stood there grinning, the two green bills in hand. A mountain of trouble would hit him until the scales of justice balanced themselves, but he would curse others for his misfortune.

I walked further into the Far Country, on the look-out for Souls worthy of the soft kiss of God. The adage,

"Many are called, but few are chosen," is as true now as it was two thousand years ago.

ECK Masters in the Silver Age, the second of the four great ages of creation, taught primitive man to build a fire and sow seeds for food. By himself, early man could not see the connection between a seed in the ground and the plant born of it.

This blindness to cause-and-effect is still man's relentless problem today. The human consciousness refuses to admit that all actions have consequences. The Living ECK Master demonstrates the Law of Balance in terms of contemporary customs.

He brings spiritual liberation, and fights to deter the ignorance that the orthodox church puts upon her people in order to contain them. The church once said that the center of the universe was earth; skeptics, such as Galileo, faced the Inquisition when they voiced their doubts about this ecclesiastical teaching.

The church further said that (1) the earth was flat; (2) that Shem, Ham, and Japheth were the ancestors of the three races in existence—the brown, black, and white—but Columbus spoiled this theory on his return from America with the discovery of the red man; and (3) that it was a sin to eat meat on Friday. Even this rule is gone now, but has anybody let old sinners out of purgatory for sins that are no longer sins today?

How can we get the God principle to come to us? Quietly sing this little prayer-song in moments of annoyance or need: "HU (Hugh)...Mahanta (mah-HON-tah)." HU is an age-old name for God, while Mahanta is a state of awareness that is beyond the Christ Consciousness.

Sing "HU...Mahanta" in a sweet, softly drawn-out breath. Do this at home or even while you are driving in traffic. In time, you will know what it means to become one with Divine Spirit.

Spiritual freedom comes when all limits of body, mind, and spirit are dissolved by the Light and Sound of God, yet the Living ECK Master pushes the divine knowledge upon no one.

Yes, you are in your rightful state of consciousness—but how much longer will you stay there?

Forever?

The king's son was digging up weeds, so that useful vegetables could grow more freely.

26

Prince or Pauper?

The tide of ECK wants to carry us into a better life, but we must first accept Its help. Spiritual paupers all, at the outset, we have only to awaken to our spiritual destiny as princes of God.

Back in the eighth century A.D., a Living ECK Master became spiritual adviser to Charlemagne, king of the Franks. This was Ketu Jaraul. Little is known of him except that he taught Charlemagne the precepts of the ECK-Vidya, the ancient science of prophecy. This ability to perceive the future was a priceless aid for the king as he steered a course through the perilous times of his reign. Ketu Jaraul's training allowed him to become a prince of ECK, instead of merely the king of an earthly realm.

On one occasion, Charlemagne learned that certain Frankish nobles planned to harm him. He was reluctant to punish them because their swords were valuable to his cause. To seek advice on how to handle the conspiracy, he sent a group of trusted men to get the opinion of his son in a distant monastery.

When the messengers arrived, they found Pepin, the son, busy in the garden, digging up weeds. They told him of the traitors and asked what to do, but Pepin refused to give advice. This distressed them greatly, because they feared the king's anger if they should return without an answer.

Soon the king's men returned home. Charlemagne began to question them closely about what Pepin had been doing during their visit.

"Just digging up weeds," they said.

"Did he say why?"

"So that useful vegetables could grow more freely in the garden," they replied. To their surprise, the king said, "You have brought back a good report."

Ketu Jaraul had opened him to the ECK-Vidya, the Golden-tongued Wisdom. Charlemagne realized that the answer he sought was embodied within the actions of his son in the garden. The Living ECK Master had shown him how the various levels of life revolve around each other like planets, each dependent upon those around them. In other words, an incident of states' importance could be understood by examining a humble incident through the special insight of ECK.

The king hesitated no longer but removed the conspirators from his sphere. The ECK-Vidya had shown him how his enemies were weeds in his kingdom, taking up high office that might better be filled with loyal supporters. That ended the problem.

Ketu Jaraul, the Living ECK Master, was responsible for the spiritual guidance of this great leader, Charlemagne. His reign is today regarded as a golden age in a time of otherwise great spiritual darkness in the West.

The golden age occurred because Charlemagne was under the direction of the Living ECK Master of the time. He was lifted from the human consciousness into the higher states of ECK, from pauper to prince.

The richness of Charlemagne's life is possible for seekers of every age. Not the material riches, but those of Spirit. The ECK-Vidya, one of the branches of ECK knowledge, gives us an understanding of a problem, but it remains for us to resolve it through use of our creative imagination. The ECK-Vidya assesses strengths we have developed in the past, strengths which can help us achieve success in this lifetime.

It is an axiom in ECK that a self-made dream is better than one created for us by another.

Here is an example of how to change the present once the ECK-Vidya has given us an insight into the reason for a problem. A few years ago I was on my way home from an ECK seminar. My plane was ready to taxi from the terminal out to the runway when it was inexplicably grounded.

The pilot on the intercom was too nonplussed to explain the delay except to say that a distant storm front had caused the air traffic controllers to reroute regional air traffic. This backed up all departures from our airport.

The ECK-Vidya opened and showed me that it was just the negative powers converging to impede my travel. So I did the following technique, which can neutralize the Kal force in many situations.

This is a visualization technique. I sat back in my seat and shut my eyes. Inwardly, I sang HU, the ancient name of God. Then, in my Spiritual Eye, I saw myself in two locations: (a) in the stranded airplane and (b) safely at the airport of my destination. Next I mocked up an image of a long-handled broom. While continuing to chant HU, I swept a clean path in my imagination between points A and B.

I then acted "as if" I were lord of my own universe. Through the inner channels, I ordered the air traffic controller to clear the flight for takeoff.

Be careful with this exercise because there is a fine line between the spiritual and psychic arts. The difference is this: Never manipulate anyone to fit your projects by invisible energy. If, however, you have entered into an agreement with an organization (such as an airline), and something there sidetracks the carrying out of your arrangement, consider it an intrusion into your psychic space by the Kal power.

Say, for instance, your travel agent gets you a ticket for a flight to another city. Your ticket is paid for, the flight is scheduled, and you are seated in the plane. In the meantime, the negative power generates a storm to stall your plane's departure. This is a valid case in which to try the spiritual exercise given above.

When not to use it: On the spur of the moment you plan to fly somewhere on vacation. At the airline counter an agent informs you the flight is sold out. Do not try to conjure up the secret forces to induce the ticket agent to find you a seat.

A prince in ECK learns to use what Paul Twitchell once called the projector (pushing) and tractor (pulling) forces. They are not a substitute for good planning.

What role then do we choose to play in life, that of prince or pauper? The ECK initiate is geared toward action, finding a creative way to solve difficulties that the spiritual paupers of this world would never consider. We are dealing with the forces of nature, learning when to step forward and when to step back. It is better to make a mistake through action than it is to be kept immobile by fear of error.

Charlemagne achieved greatness for himself and his countrymen because he learned about the ebb and flow of ECK. He was able to put his knowledge to use for the betterment of many.

The fears and opportunities that he faced are no greater or less than any you must face in your own spiritual worlds. All that is expected of the God seeker is that he conquer himself. You, like Charlemagne, have the help of the Living ECK Master of the times. If you qualify, the ECK-Vidya can become a real asset in your spiritual life.

The challenge remains: Will you be the prince of God, or remain a pauper? The difference between them is as simple as the ancient song of HU.

And that is up to you.

The seed of fortune, or awareness, allowed Alexander to ride the horse.

27

Seed of Fortune

Our unfoldment is along three lines: learning, growing, and knowing. They tie together the past, present, and future.

An old story is told of Alexander the Great when he was a boy. His father, King Philip II of Macedon, bought a fiery, young horse that had cost him his own weight in silver. The problem was that no one could ride it.

The king turned the horse over to a soldier who had trained horses for years. The horse bucked him off time and again. Philip admired the noble animal, but it was useless as a war-horse without training. The soldier said to the king, "There is nothing I can do to make this a war-horse. It is better to be rid of it."

Alexander had just finished his lessons for the day with Aristotle, his famous tutor. He watched the soldier's futile attempts to ride the wild horse. When he heard the soldier advise the king to be rid of the animal, Alexander ran up to them and said, "Let me. I can ride him!" The two warriors laughed at the boy. After all, if an experienced horseman could not stay on the horse, what could a schoolboy do?

"If you can ride him," said Philip, "he's yours."

Alexander took the rope from the soldier and talked quietly to the horse. Soon it settled down, the terror out of its eyes. In a flash, the boy leapt upon its back and the horse took off in a gallop. After a long run it accepted the boy on its back, so Alexander headed home.

The king was astonished to see the boy and horse thunder up in a cloud of dust. "Is he really mine?" asked Alexander wistfully.

"He is, if you'll tell me what you did to ride him when no one else could."

"You've always told me to observe things with care," said Alexander, "then use the information learned to solve the problem."

"That's right."

"I noticed that the soldier turned his back to the sun. This threw the horse's shadow on the ground in front of him. But he was afraid of his shadow, so I faced him into the sun, calmed him down, then mounted him. When he was tired of running, I turned toward home. Now his shadow didn't frighten him anymore, even though the sun was to his back."

Alexander had the seed of awareness inside him. He was able to see the reason for the horse's fear, which his father and the soldier could not. So King Philip gave him the horse.

The seed of fortune, or awareness, put in Alexander's care was later misused for conquest, which he thought would bring peace of Soul. Instead it led to his untimely death. His search for happiness was in vain, despite all his victories in battle. Most ECK initiates today know the spiritual laws better than Alexander did. The seed of fortune entrusted to them is used to feed spiritual, not material hungers.

The story of Alexander was from the past; now let's look closer to the present for the seed of fortune, which is the gift of consciousness. The following incident took place last October at the ECK Worldwide Seminar in St. Louis, Missouri.

A student, who had begun his study of ECK just the previous spring, went to the HU Chant before the regular Sunday morning program. As he joined in the chant, he found himself in the Soul body, drifting toward a vortex of light. This vortex was beneath another huge vortex that must have spread across billions upon billions of miles. Both had the appearance of tornadoes.

Strong power pulsed in the smaller vortex, but he summoned up his courage and went through its swirling mass. There he found a magnificent city, which was like a hollow cylinder standing on end, with many levels to it. Each level contained lights, trees, and plants, as well as other Souls.

He was on a balcony somewhere on the inner rim of the vertical city. Leaning over a railing, he looked up and down the vast open hub of the city. Then he remembered the large vortex above. From it descended a platform in the shape of a half-moon that stopped on his level. Two spiritual beings were talking nearby, and he overheard one say, "Another one is being initiated."

Next, he was on the platform, in a circle of light. He looked out from the light and saw the ECK Spiritual Travelers—Wah Z, Peddar Zaskq, and Rebazar Tarzs—who stood around him smiling. The platform rose up through the smaller vortex and entered into the larger.

Suddenly, Blue Light shot at him from all sides, covering and almost blinding him with Its intensity. This was the Blue Light of the Mahanta. The Light

175

dimmed in a few minutes, and he could again see the Masters, who stood before him.

Wah Z greeted him with open arms, hugged him, and said, "You will learn."

Peddar Zaskq (Paul Twitchell) hugged him and said, "You will grow."

Rebazar Tarzs, hugging him, said, "You will know."

The neophyte was returned almost immediately to the seminar HU Chant when the MC there ended the chant with the words, "May the blessings be."

This was the initiate's seed of fortune. It was the true ECK initiation, the gift of consciousness. Now he must see to it that the seed bears fruit. Already he is aware of being in the higher awareness of ECK when talking with others or doing his job. The seed of fortune is knowing that the Mahanta is always with him. This is the Face of the Master that shines in all whom he meets.

He now has the initial linkup with ECK, the Sound Current of old. Like Alexander in the past, he will learn by observation, but will reach beyond intellectual learning. As in his experience at the ECK seminar in the present, he will grow via the ECK initiations. And in the future, he will know by means of the Golden-tongued Wisdom. This is the ECK-Vidya, the ancient science of prophecy.

The Golden-tongued Wisdom means just that: the ECK lights up certain bits of information in conversation or print that other people do not catch. That's why it's called "Golden-tongued." This is the ECK-Vidya in one of its many forms. The key to understanding these cues for the better handling of our lives is in the seed of fortune—awareness, which is opened through the Spiritual Exercises of ECK and initiation.

Even Chinese fortune cookies can be used by the ECK to give one the Golden-tongued Wisdom. But don't trust them blindly, for once the Mahanta begins to instruct Soul, Its affairs go outside the ring of fate, which is the literal level of the fortunes. You can accept and enjoy fortune slips that build your spiritual character, but absolutely reject those that limit or threaten you.

A Chinese fortune cookie has in it a seed, a fortune. Some fortunes tell you how to conduct yourself, others are promises or warnings for the future. Look for the uplifting messages. For instance, "A new chapter in your life is being written" may alert you to an important personal change. "Whatever arrangements you make are apt to be final" could be a warning to carefully rethink some plan in the works, because of its long-lasting influence.

Some messages just make good sense. "When you go out to buy, don't show your silver." That's the Law of Economy. A good spiritual reminder is this one, which demonstrates the returns of love: "If you continually give, you will continually have." Fortunes we all like include: "Your life will be happy and peaceful," "Many ideals are becoming real," and "Your present plans are going to succeed."

Fortune cookies are one of the lighter sides of the ECK-Vidya, and the ECK may choose the humble fortune cookie to prod your awareness. Any ECK initiate who has the seed of fortune (awareness) can easily read its real meaning. The Mahanta's guidance is without limits, but the ECKist must be able to see it.

The seed of fortune contains the enigmatic riddle of "the three, in the three, in the three." The past, present, and future; learn, grow, and know; and the individual, the Mahanta, and SUGMAD.

Where is your seed of fortune?

When an oil well belonging to the church began to produce, supplicants felt it their religious right to be given some of the profits. The human condition hardly misses a beat, for it always expects to get something for nothing.

28

Eye of the Tiger

The Delaware Indians, who originally came from the eastern woodlands of North America, initiated the boys of the tribe into manhood by a rite called the Youth's Vigil.

When a boy reached puberty and was ready for the greater role of the warrior-in-training, he was made to go alone into the forest and fast for many days. It was to test his bravery, but also to let him see that nature, while a harsh teacher of those ignorant of its ways, was also a supportive force that would help the individual who would listen to its whispers.

The ordeal of fasting and solitude in the forest was to open the youth's Third Eye and let him wander from then on in the land of dreams and prophecies. They would be his guide for all the years to follow when he would be an honored brave among his people.

Soul is much like the Delaware Indian boy. It too is put into a climate of instruction where It sees the need for a great awakening.

The *eye of the tiger* thus means this: It is the look in the eye of a person who is qualified by the trials in life

179

to act in his own best spiritual interests. He makes his life aright, routing problems that once paralyzed him on the road to God. No more is he the sluggard, who takes a feeble swipe at trouble, but then clasps his hands in bitter defeat and says, "I let the ECK do it, but It doesn't work."

It is apparent to a student of human nature that the spiritual decline of man in society is here without a question. The old ideals of courage, independence, and strength are on the wane among people on the street. Reliance upon the inner Self is weak, and so is much of one's outer self-rule. Anybody in his right mind tries to get as much "free" help from our grandfatherly government as possible. And it is deemed a "right" for one to do that.

Where do you, the ECK initiate, fit into this unreal picture of our society? How do you adjust to life in a setting where dependency upon others is the standard? How on earth does Soul keep Its vision on the Kingdom of God when Its back is bent among the slaves of materialism?

The individual with the eye of the tiger is a leader who walks toward trouble that wants to paralyze him. He has gotten the formula for ECK Mastership. Now he acts to work through the secrets of the future, bringing into the present moment the fruit of his creative imagination, which is the birth of all spiritual unfoldment.

Two classes of consciousness make up the people around us: the awakened and the sleeping. The awakened move to the Light and Sound of ECK brought to them by the Mahanta, but the sleeping prefer to live off the labors of others. The latter are like the male honeybee, which is a parasite on the worker bee; fittingly, it has no sting.

180

A Soul that is idle in the fields of earth, as It once was in the gardens of heaven, is like a bee with no sting. It is in a useless incarnation and must return to earth in another lifetime.

The sleeping ones do not have the eye of the tiger. Nor do they know what it is and would not know it if they saw it. They are the drones who will not permit anyone to awaken them for the coming of the Mahanta, who can bring Light and Sound to the silence of darkness.

Most people are nonproducers and become very angry if told that. Envy and covetousness are their creed, and the passion for even more possessions is a full-time activity. Malice, negativity, and gossip are kept close at hand. They are the takers instead of the givers in life. Misery and unhappy situations trail them from the crib to the tomb.

Only the Mahanta, the Living ECK Master has the ability to stop the downhill fall of today's spiritual decline. He is the sole agent with the spiritual power to establish a new golden age, to turn the momentum of the negative forces into the spiritual ones. Chosen initiates are put into training to tell the prisoners of Kal that only one key unlocks their cells: the Spiritual Exercises of ECK.

The Mahanta's message to Soul is the reality of spiritual liberation in this lifetime. Who other than the Mahanta can lift one above himself?

Most people do not want to be in charge of their own survival but want other people or agencies to support them. A recent *Time* magazine news item told about a country church in southern Illinois that had for years depended upon donations from the collection plate to pay its bills. But a piece of land willed to the church years ago brought in a well that spewed oil in the amount of $10,000 every month.

The windfall to the church coffers brought a problem. A flood of requests came from supplicants who wanted handouts for everything from paying the rent to fixing the roof. To compound the problem, a second well also began to produce oil, doubling the income.

The supplicants are an example of people who had done nothing to earn the money, but who felt it a religious right to be given some of it. The human condition hardly misses a beat, for it always expects to get something for nothing.

What I'm saying is this: All who expect to get to heaven must do something to get there. The uncomfortable truth in ECK is that not everybody will get to heaven in this life span. The takers, those who are the sleeping ones, have not done the spiritual exercises at all, or not long enough to realize the initial awakening of the spiritual Self.

The man who sees with the eye of the tiger finds a wealth of chances for growth despite the checkmates played against him. The hum of the ECK Sound Current stirs up his desire to be a Co-worker with God. Human desires, however, have to crumble before the greater love of Soul can give service to something beyond and more lasting than the self.

Man in the human predicament is a victim of the Law of Likes. The Shariyat identifies him as one who looks for materialistic solutions to problems, and thus attracts to him people who are materialists.

On the other hand, an initiate who is free of the destructive traits of the mind draws to him those individuals who are of a spiritual nature.

The way to heaven is told to us in the Shariyat-Ki-Sugmad, but the actual working out of this high destiny is done in the privacy of your contemplation.

By all means, do what you are able to do toward self-sufficiency, but do not get off welfare if you need it to live on. The idea is to make a *gradual* change from dependency to independence. Start to think how you can do even one little thing to become a self-reliant person over the long haul.

There would be no point to this article if I left you feeling either a sense of guilt or unable to survive without aid in the circumstances you are in today. The point is: First, change your thinking, then make a gradual effort to care for yourself in both the material and spiritual worlds.

Do accept all the Mahanta's help that is given to you, however, until you reach this state of self-mastery.

My neighbor insisted on taking what he called a short-cut, but each time I arrived at a rest stop before him.

29

The Law of Gratitude

The Law of Gratitude states simply that abundance flourishes in a grateful heart.

A certain ECK initiate travels extensively at home and abroad. In her travels, she has observed that a large number of people have the satisfaction of a comfortable life, but a great many others live hand to mouth.

She wondered why she had the right set of circumstances to study ECK while so many others did not. What had she done to deserve the freedom of the spiritual life? Was it that these others were victims of their own karma, simply reaping the due rewards for what they had sown in the past? She didn't know.

While travel gave her the awareness not to become smug with good fortune, what, she wondered, could offset complacency?

In a word: gratitude.

At the turn of the century, there lived a man in the midwestern United States who was pursued by poverty. He devised every sort of scheme in order to provide a comfortable living for his family; but his schemes generally failed.

This was Wallace D. Wattles, author of *The Science of Getting Rich*. In it, he outlined a singular approach for achieving a life of abundance. The ideas in this book often parallel the spiritual concepts of Paul Twitchell in *The Flute of God*. It is therefore worthy of consideration.

Wattles's repeated failures caused him to take a long, hard look at himself. Why did other men succeed when their abilities were no greater than his own? He began to study the philosophies of Descartes, Spinoza, Emerson, and others. He came to accept the monistic principle of "One Substance" as being responsible for all creation. Taking this a step further, he guessed that this impartial force, if addressed correctly, would provide him with the full abundance of life.

We know this force as the ECK Power. On the Mental Plane, It acts through the Universal Mind Power. This latter force is neutral, like the pure force of ECK; but unlike the ECK, it is highly unstable. Our minds are of the same inconstant matter. Yet are they not wonderful instruments of ECK when rightly used?

From the first day that Wattles discovered the ECK Current, until his untimely death in 1911, he would form a strong mental picture of whatever he desired. He then did realize his dream of attaining an abundant life, through the power of visualization. He knew that this Master Force would always give a rightful share of the good things to those with a grateful, knowing heart.

But yet, once the ECK grants us Its blessings, how often do we remember to acknowledge them? Acknowledgment is done through gratitude, which keeps our hearts open to ECK. When gratitude is lost, the result is spiritual poverty.

Gratitude appears in subtle ways. Once I went to a schoolroom on the inner planes to watch children learning arithmetic. The teacher asked a bright-eyed boy, "If you had one tomato and needed ten, how many more would you have to buy?"

The boy thought a moment then said, "None! I'd cut open my tomato, plant the seeds, and grow *many* tomatoes." The teacher, impressed by the boy's ingenuity, accepted the answer. The boy had an appreciation for life that let him view it more fully than others.

The point is that creative people who cherish the gift of life often slip into the secret chambers of the creative mind. Their solutions are well-rounded, more sensible than those of people who rely solely upon reason as their mainstay. Gratitude unseals fountains of creativity, because a grateful person is relaxed. This allows him to take stock of his circumstances with an objective mind. Like the boy in the story, a creative person often gets three-dimensional answers to his problems.

Creativity, bountifulness, and gratitude thus go hand in hand.

The ECK will give us all that we need. First we must learn to expect the best in life, and be willing to plan and work for it. Second, we need a clear mental picture of what we desire. Third, this picture is to be maintained constantly, with the certainty that ECK will supply any rightful desire. Fourth, there must be gratitude for every good thing received.

It was in such a way that the ECK helped my family years ago. In 1975, the ECKANKAR Office was to move from Las Vegas, Nevada, to Menlo Park, California. Management had arranged to rent trucks for the staff to move themselves. However, the goods on the trucks would be unavailable to their owners for several days because of travel and storage complications.

Our daughter was not yet eighteen months old, so her crib, playpen, and high chair had to go with us by car. This meant towing a trailer, but regrettably, we did not have money to rent one.

Then I used the method above.

A few evenings before my wife and I were to leave Nevada, we took a farewell drive in Las Vegas and came upon a community bingo parlor. Responding to a nudge from the Inner Master, we stopped to play a game. Much to our surprise, we both won. Our winnings were just enough to cover the rental of the trailer. The ECK fulfilled our need through this happy means.

 Gratitude for gifts we have already received sets into motion new forces that sustain a life of fullness. A grateful person usually finds the windows of spiritual opportunity open to him.

Once, while in the Far Country, I elected to guide a neighbor to a distant location. The cross-country journey led through marshes, cold mountain streams, and other rugged terrain. Periodically this fellow groused because I kept to the trail. He wanted to leave it and take a shortcut. Each time I said, "The trail is faster."

At length he got disgusted with the rate of our progress and set off by himself. He thought he could make better time alone because he was physically stronger than me. But I knew the treacheries of the land.

So he jogged off out of sight. Our paths crossed often, since I was watching out for him. Each time I arrived at a rest stop before him, he became increasingly more agitated. He was constantly running into dead ends and wasting valuable time and energy. His determination to arrive first at our destination became more fierce at each rest point.

It was a journey of countless obstacles. Tiredness overcame him, this newcomer to the Far Country. He began to discard his equipment, but he left it strewn on other people's land. As his guide, I was responsible for

188

the litter. So I picked up the abandoned gear—cooking utensils, walking stick, even his canteen. They were to assist, not hamper, my own journey.

The trail was familiar to me so it was possible to travel at leisure. From the discarded supplies, I was able to make a cup of tea before his arrival at each rest camp. The camping gear that had burdened him was my boon.

Eventually he safely reached journey's end, but he was weary from the conflict with his ego. His discord, he thought, was caused by my determination to stick to the trail when he thought it unnecessary. Regardless, it was really his private struggle with the competitiveness of his own mind; I was borne along by the spirit of gratitude.

Life will be more rewarding when we learn the secret of gratitude. Wattles finally learned this in his later years. One who is thankful for every good thing will find the richness of heaven in the humblest detail of his spiritual life.

The window of gratitude opens to us the heavens of God.

All too often, we play the game of life like a cat with an unruly tail.

30

It's All in the Game

One day I watched Sunny, our neighbor's orange cat, from my living-room window. Evidently, a mouse had been rustling in the tall grass beyond our backyard. Stealthily, Sunny inched forward, ever so carefully, every muscle alert to pounce on his prey.

Ten minutes later, Sunny was still only half his length into the tall grass. It looked as if he were doing everything right: his ears perked to hear the slightest movement of the mouse; his movement, slow and careful; and his strong desire to catch the mouse. But Sunny was unwittingly working against himself.

The closer he got to the mouse, the more excited he became. In his growing excitement his tail took on a life of its own, thrashing wildly against the high grass. But Sunny seemed blissfully unaware of his tail betraying him.

Finally, he made a great leap, but came away empty. The mouse had made it to safety.

All too often, we play the game of life like a cat with an unruly tail. Our desire for God is worthy, but we do not have the discipline to reach our goal.

A small bug was walking very close to the wall outside my bathroom window. It approached the corner, not aware that a spider had spun its webs there. The bug ran into a web. This alerted the spider, who was waiting above, clinging to one of the delicate silken threads. The spider glided down his ladder to land behind the bug and inspect it, then shot back up to his overview. A second later, the spider descended to attack, this time landing on top of the bug.

In an explosion of desperate motion, the two met. Just as quickly, the spider again climbed to his vantage point. The bug lay still. It appeared the spider had poisoned his quarry.

The bug had been trudging along minding its own business, until it blundered into the hunting ground of the spider. This nearly cost the bug its life, the error coming to a head in a brief but fierce encounter. After the attack, the bug seemed defeated. For a while it lay still, but it was only gathering strength. In a short time the bug stirred. It got up, made a few false starts in the direction of where the spiderweb was thickest, but then slowly retraced a part of its original route until clear of danger. Then it continued on to its original destination. This time, however, the bug took a shortcut and bypassed the spider's lair. One visit was enough.

<u>We usually try to do what's right, but experience teaches us to do it better.</u>

An ECKist found herself at dinner with a new acquaintance, a woman in a class she was taking. The chela had plans to go to an ECK meeting that night, and without thinking, she mentioned it to her acquaintance, who turned out to be a born-again Christian. The woman had no regard for anyone with values other than her own. She hit the initiate with a barrage of questions, which the latter attempted to answer, though she knew it would serve no useful end. The dinner was ruined and likely also their friendship.

Soon after that unhappy event, the ECKist got an abscessed tooth. The pain continued to get worse, even after the dentist had pulled the tooth. He explained that it was a "dry socket," a condition where no scab develops over the wound. Thus food or liquid go straight to the bone.

The ECKist understood that the pain in her mouth was due to "mouthing off" to her acquaintance. In the future, she plans to use better judgment in a one-on-one chat about ECKANKAR. If people are curiosity seekers, she will tell them, "It's a study of spiritual principles." And if they continue to ply her with questions, she'll add, "It's too much to explain in a few minutes. If you really want to know and are not just being polite, I'll get a book to you."

Such is the game of life.

And so also for a young man who is learning the game of spiritual survival from yet another slant. Most ECKists get into trouble when they tell companions about the far worlds of God. He does just the opposite. He Soul Travels to the other worlds and tells people there about earth. They may be just as much in the dark about Soul Travel and the Sound and Light of God as people here. But it is all in the line of unfoldment.

Still, he too is learning important lessons. During Soul Travel to a new place, he asks people the name of their city. Then he tells them where he comes from and how he got there. When they ask about ECKANKAR and the Mahanta, he offers to call the Master if they wish to meet him. Usually Wah Z appears to greet them.

But here is where this individual is confronting his own lessons. He has a habit of snapping his fingers when he wants the Master to appear, but the Mahanta is really the ECK. On occasion, Wah Z has brought him up short by saying, "I'll see you later." The chela still thinks the ECK, or the Holy Spirit, is something to order around. Yet It cannot be pushed, for ECK sustains all of life itself.

 The chela has only to open himself as a channel for ECK. It will decide what is to be done or not. This is all part of learning the game of life.

Why is it some do well in ECK, while others find it hard to realize any spiritual advancement? The key for success or failure is ultimately within ourself.

A Higher Initiate told of a recent dream that gave the reason he was not remembering his inner experiences. In the dream, he and his wife were on a Ferris wheel that rose higher and higher into the sky. Soon he realized they were no longer on the amusement ride, but were passing from plane to plane. Ever higher they flew. He was still in the seat, but more than a bit afraid of the great height. Finally, unable to take it any longer, he covered his eyes. His wife said, "You can't see like that." To which he replied, "I know, but I'm afraid to look."

When he awoke, he found the dream experience amusing. And now he knows why he cannot recall many of his inner experiences: He is afraid to look. It is a good start toward understanding.

The game of life is to help us understand how ECK works in our lives. One day, a woman lost patience with her husband, who was being unusually stubborn. With a sigh, she said, "You have come to teach me patience." He thought a moment, then replied, "And you have come to teach me love." At least, now they know. The ECK is making each a better, more spiritual being through the other.

Later, she had a wonderful insight: "So, in a way, the most difficult person in our life is also an assignment from the SUGMAD."

Whether cat, bug, or human, we are all learning physical or spiritual survival. It is all in the game.

The Indian and the pony were "a single unit in mind, heart, body, and purpose." That's how Soul must become with ECK.

31

Odyssey of Soul

Soul gets spiritual freedom by passing through three seasons in Its journey to God: (1) innocence, (2) complication, and (3) fulfillment. The passage of Soul is as sure as the sun's; and through the morning, noon, and eventide of life's experience, It climbs steadily up the rugged mountainside to God-Realization.

But the climb is torturous. Grief, loneliness, hunger, and disease sour the drink of life. We want God, but this spiritual odyssey takes us to unknown places in the far worlds of consciousness. But of all things learned, nothing is more necessary than how to become one with the ECK, a Co-worker with God.

Parables of Soul's uncertain passage through the three states named above are in the library. An example is *The Count of Monte Cristo,* a classic tale of adventure by Alexandre Dumas that illustrates Soul's turbulent migration from innocence to refinement; from inexperience to power; and then, to the joy of love.

The story is about you and me in the person of a young sailor named Edmond Dantès. The full beauty and wonder of life is before him at nineteen. He is in line

197

for promotion to captain of a merchant ship, which is unusual for one so young, and which will make him a well-to-do husband for his fiancée. But treachery spins the wheel of fortune, and he lands in prison. An old monk tells him of a fabulous treasure, and when Dantès escapes, he finds it.

He now assumes the identity of the Count of Monte Cristo, but all the wealth in the world cannot repay the years of suffering in prison, nor restore his aged father, who starved to death in his absence. His weak-willed fiancée has long since married the rival who helped betray him to the public prosecutor.

Dantès is no longer a naive orphan in life but becomes the dreadful avenger. Like him, we, as the inexperienced Soul, opt for power to hold our own. We enter the second part of our spiritual training and embrace the merciless philosophy of "an eye for an eye." Dantès eventually sickens of the carnage he causes those who wronged him, and he lays aside the sword of reprisal. Thus he abandons the second phase of Soul's education, a complicated life of futility.

Now he enters the final stage of fulfillment, or realization. You and I, like Dantès, want to stop the senseless battles that destroy all in our wake. By now, Soul has gained some degree of mastery over Itself and is hungry for the Sound and Light of God. The rounds of experience in all things of life give It a ticket to find the path of ECK, which is the original teaching of the Holy Spirit for mankind.

Dantès, in the season of realization, suddenly understands why there is pain and suffering. In the state of spiritual balance he has acquired through all his experience, he realizes this secret of God: "There is neither happiness nor unhappiness in this world; there is only the comparison of one state with another. Only

198

a man who has felt ultimate despair is capable of feeling ultimate bliss." Likewise, an immature Soul is incapable of God Consciousness.

Life is nothing more than Soul meeting Itself in the reflection of the outer world. Beyond the pages of a novel, It can only reap what It sows.

In *Kinship with All Life,* J. Allen Boone repeats the saying of the ECK Masters that "thoughts are things." Boone recounts meeting an old prospector who told him that rattlesnakes took "special delight in sinking their fangs into a white man," but they seldom harmed an Indian.

Boone concluded that the reptile reacts to the different thought patterns sent out by the two men. The white man is taught from childhood to fear the serpent (a throwback to the Garden of Eden). The snake appraises the kind of thinking that is moving in its direction and is ready to deal with either friend or foe. The snake is highly sensitive to any mental poison and quickly poisons its own state of consciousness in response. The snake truly reflects the enemy's thoughts, and it's an encounter without quarter.

The real Indian, however, regards a wild creature as a much-loved younger brother. When he comes into the area of this same snake, he pauses. The two contemplate each other, "like a big and small ship at sea exchanging friendly messages." The Indian, Boone said, was taught to move in harmony with what he called the Big Holy. We call this the ECK, or Holy Spirit.

The odyssey of Soul teaches us to cooperate with the laws of God. It takes many lifetimes of bumps and bruises before all the lessons of Godhood sink in. And when they do, we are granted the grace to partake consciously of the highest aspects of sainthood.

The loving relationship between the ECK and you, a spark of God, is well told by another example from Boone. As a boy, he was spellbound by pictures of Indians riding their ponies without bridles, saddles, or blankets. Later he watched Indians perform the same feat in Buffalo Bill's Wild West Show. It was not clear how they could stay on their ponies while making sudden turns at high speed.

Finally, he got to ask a chief how the Indians were able to ride bareback so well. In sign language, the chief said that there was a "friendly and understanding contact between Indian and pony." All their interests were interrelated. The Indian and the pony were "a single unit in mind, heart, body, and purpose." That's how Soul must become with ECK.

We are in a peculiar conflict while in this body. Most living things try to keep alive at all costs. But as Schopenhauer, the nineteenth-century German philosopher, observed, when "existence is assured," people don't know what to do with it. So they try to free themselves from "the burden of existence, to make it cease to be felt, 'to kill time.' "

This is a case of Soul in the second stage, the stage of complication, spoken of before. Being freed of want and care, almost all such people become a burden to themselves. This boredom opens the door to the social consciousness, which drives "men to the greatest excesses, as much as its opposite extreme, famine."

The individual in the third stage is well poised between desire and its attainment. By long experience, he has seen the advantage of controlling the transmissions of his thoughts into the world. In short, he has attained the detached state of the God-Conscious individual.

The odyssey of Soul is worth every sacrifice, for it leads to God.

The ECK initiate is a step ahead of Maugham's aviator, who thought he had to go to India to find spiritual realization.

32

The Razor's Edge

A wonderful story by Somerset Maugham, the popular English author of the early to mid-twentieth century, tells of the conflicts of a searcher for God.

Found in most libraries, *The Razor's Edge* follows the life of a World War I aviator whose friend gave his life in an air battle to save him. But the battle he never speaks of is the one between the spiritual and the social consciousness, yet it forces him to make a decision at the crossroads, not once, but many times. He has returned to America with no taste for the wealth and materialism that America is hungering for.

The individual in ECK is continually confronted by the Razor's Edge. The Mahanta puts him to repeated tests, waiting to see which is of more importance to him—the ECK or the tarnished allure of society.

In an earnest conversation with Maugham, the aviator takes to task the social God, whom people believed wanted to be worshiped. He talks of his stay at a monastery where the monks could give no answers to quiet his questions. Why would an all-powerful God want worship? Why did He create evil? What kind of a God would construct a soiled universe and then blame an angel for the trouble in it, when God, with all His power, could have stopped the Dark Angel at will?

The aviator had locked horns with the failings of this social God, a creation of the human consciousness. The values of that God's children, including his fiancée's, were plastic tokens substituted for gold coins. His fiancée wanted the latest fashions from Paris; he wanted the freedom to search for truth, to travel to find it. She wished to drink of the social whirl; he, of the consciousness of God.

Unable to agree on a common goal, they broke their engagement. This was one of a number of painful decisions made by Maugham's hero at the crossroads—the spiritual versus the social consciousness.

Keen observation by the aviator revealed the fear people suffer. It was not fear of closed spaces or heights that he saw in them, but fear of death; worse yet, fear of life. This fear afflicted people "in the best of health, prosperous, without any [other apparent] worry."

The social consciousness is generally the starting place for most people who come to ECK. The spiritual exercises lift them toward the higher state as they enter into the higher initiations.

Walt Whitman, one of America's greatest poets and an old man when Maugham was a youth, was another truth seeker who could only rebel at the values of the social consciousness. His *Leaves of Grass* can be regarded as scripture, but when this book of poetry was published in 1855, critics savagely attacked it. Whitman, they charged, was "as unacquainted with art as a hog is with mathematics."

No doubt, Whitman inflamed society because of his celebrated ideas of sexuality, ideas that would be quite tame by today's standards. Ever the advocate of individual freedom, he took sharp jabs at the God of society in "Song of Myself," one of the poems in *Leaves of Grass*.

He was of the bemused opinion that he could "turn and live awhile with the animals." They did not lie awake at night and weep for their sins; they did not complain about their condition. Nor did the animals make him sick by discussing their duty to God. They had no desire to own anything. Further, animals did not bow to each other, especially to one of their kind that had lived thousands of years ago.

Whitman spent most of his life on the Razor's Edge, trying to keep a line of separation between the call of Soul in him and the insanity of the spiritually dead outside.

The ECK initiate is a step ahead of Maugham's aviator, who thought he had to go to India to find spiritual realization. The ECKist is also further along in unfoldment than Whitman, if he knows how foolish it is to anger those in the human consciousness by making fun of the God of their own creation.

The Razor's Edge is one's calm detachment from the things of this world; yet he may enjoy them as a blessing of life, for past karma has brought them for his experience. There is no virtue in suffering, poverty, or martyrdom, unless the individual needs those experiences for the purification of Soul.

Participants at an ECKANKAR seminar were asked to tell why they were in ECKANKAR. One of the individuals expressed the spirit of the aviator and Whitman. When he did things for himself, it seemed to benefit others. He wanted the freedom to make his own mistakes and could not tolerate the constraint of any kind of outside order.

His opinion of how to live the spiritual life is close. I would add that it's not the things done for the little self that work out well for others, but those things that are done for the greater principle, the ECK or the SUGMAD. The Razor's Edge of discrimination always hounds a seeker of God.

Another chela said the past year had been a catharsis, a cleansing, for him. A series of traumatic things happened to him that ended in his surrender to the Inner Master. He found that he had to be knocked about first before he could learn surrender.

A businessman reported real resistance to the ECK, although he was unaware of it in himself. He acknowledged that a lot of changes have taken place since he's been in ECK, but he hasn't decided yet whether it was the ECK or not. He has more detachment with his clients, but he'd rather take the credit for this himself, as a personal accomplishment.

A former teacher is doing well with the Razor's Edge, which, after all, is nothing more than the line between self-service and God-service. She asks new people, "What can I tell you?" Usually, they aren't asking her to talk, but to listen. So she listens: God-service.

The blade of the Razor's Edge cuts two ways: it can make one great or destroy him. The tests are given in ways not always seen by the individual. He is asked to make a choice between the approval of others, or the Mahanta. If he chooses correctly, his life will be changed from that moment on, even if he does not realize he has been tested by the Master. I could give examples of this, but the experience is too personal to those who have met the Razor's Edge. The decision pits the higher and lower selves against each other, and the answer that comes out of this conflict either adds or subtracts karma—a gain or loss in spirituality.

Decisions made at thousands of different crossroads have led Soul to the Mahanta. For some the way is quicker than for others; it all depends upon Soul's desire to find the principle of divine love that we call the ECK. But when the chela comes to the final crossroad and chooses to follow the Inner Master, a meeting between the two is assured.

How is your balance on the Razor's Edge?

This woman mentioned ECK to a friend at work and did so without understanding why, for she does not press her interests upon others. She was conducting herself as a clear vehicle for Spirit.

33

Carriers of Truth

The outflow that comes from giving of oneself opens the door to spiritual unfoldment while the attitude of taking locks it. Yet the Mahanta never encourages austerities of any kind.

Those with knowledge of the Eternal, says *The Shariyat-Ki-Sugmad,* are men and women who enjoy life so much that they risk being immersed completely in it. The company of these individuals includes the ECK Masters, whose intensity of love has always been directed toward service to God.

The struggle between giving and taking is illustrated in the case of a conscientious seeker who joined a particular religious group. He devoted himself to its program and advanced at a steady rate, for he wanted to give service while absorbing every conceivable lesson available.

On the side, he began to earn income through voluntary assistance in furthering the program; not a lot of money, but enough to defray expenses. Reluctant to put a price on his time, he nevertheless accepted little gifts for his volunteer work. The real, but unrecognized, reward that flowed in from all directions was personal unfoldment.

Then came the fork in the road. Some of the older, more worldly-wise instructors counseled him to charge more money for his valuable time. On the surface their advice seemed plausible: "As an advanced Soul and teacher, you should not run all over the country for a few dollars."

This person, like most ECKists, loves life. He turned away from the path of giving to that of taking, for Soul required the experience. This is not to say that one cannot be paid for honest work, but with his changed attitude of taking instead of giving he started to put a price upon his gift to God. Before long he dropped out of this religious group because the enjoyment was gone.

Searching for the next step in his spiritual life, he joined ECKANKAR. Unfortunately, with him came the old attitude: "What can the ECK do for me?" rather than, "What can I do for the ECK?"

Nor did his job interest him any longer, for the joy of growing was now reduced to the consideration: How much could he earn? Working more and more overtime, he nevertheless fell deeper into debt.

One day he saw that he no longer needed this experience and that his troubles had sprung from nothing other than constantly taking from life without returning anything to it. Absorbing this subtle lesson, he reversed the downhill slide in consciousness and started to give of himself again.

A woman who had somewhat learned to give of herself but was reluctant to declare herself a vehicle because Spirit might ask for talents she lacked, did so anyway during a major ECKANKAR seminar in Chicago. Somebody asked her to drive two people downtown. Confident in her driving ability, she found this an agreeable task. Would she loan her cassette deck for a portion of the program? Certainly! Moving a step further, she volunteered the audio experience she had learned in broadcasting school; the seminar staff gratefully accepted her expertise. Each small step in giving led to another.

Willing to share her talents, she concluded, "All the ECK wanted me to do when I offered to help was to do the things I already knew how to do! This is not to say I was not challenged. I had a great opportunity to grow along the way."

A gift to Spirit must be rendered without thought of reward. The uninitiated are waiting for news of ECK, and their first step could well be the gift of an ECK book placed in an airport, on a bus, or in a laundromat. Each and every ECKist has a specific purpose to spread the message of ECK, working in the sphere where he can be of most use to others. Becoming a Co-worker with God begins in the simplest of ways.

A lady wrote that she mentioned ECK to a friend at work and did so without understanding why she brought up the topic, for she does not press her interests upon others. Her acquaintance proved "very interested in the works and completely devoured all the books I gave her on the subject." This woman was conducting herself as a clear vehicle for Spirit, for It saw someone ready to hearken to Its majestic voice and had already prepared the way.

Initiates in an Austrian town had scheduled an ECK introductory talk for the local Pythagoras/Kepler School. Since several scientists planned to attend, the ECKists prepared themselves in areas concerning Pythagoras and Kepler.

In the meantime the lecture was switched from the school to a local bank. The scientists did not arrive, but of the forty-four people in attendance, half were new to ECKANKAR. After the ECK books had been introduced to the audience, the young visitors, mostly members of a local church, engaged the ECKists in an earnest and enthusiastic discussion on the main points of ECK.

The initiate who maintains a balance between giving and taking can be an effective carrier of the Everlasting Gospel of ECK.

The Living ECK Master links Soul with the heavenly Sound Current that flows from God's great center into the worlds below. This vast wave, called the ECK, touches all beings and leads finally to the dwelling place of the SUGMAD.

The spiritual new year for ECKANKAR begins on October 22, the date commemorating the passing of the Rod of ECK Power.

34

Working Together in ECK

The spiritual new year for ECKANKAR begins on October 22, the date commemorating the passing of the Rod of ECK Power. We have entered a time of spiritual renewal. Again, there is a quickening of the Life pulse. This is the moment for the individual who wishes to become a Co-worker with God to take stock of where he stands on this most direct path to the SUGMAD.

"We in ECK are more interested in seeing the chela become himself, rather than someone else," says *The Spiritual Notebook*. This same observation was made by an ECKist, who said, "When one becomes a Higher Initiate, he becomes more himself, instead of perfect." As we unfold into the higher states of consciousness, we realize that with the greater spiritual freedom comes increased responsibility.

Every ECKist is aware of the spiritual law that everything must be paid for in the true coin. This means that we are, in a spiritual sense, going to have to earn our unfoldment in some manner or another. The key to this is contained in the four fundamentals of ECK: the

215

first is self-discipline. Then, the absolute inner reliance on the Mahanta. Third, the Spiritual Exercises of ECK; and, finally, the true contemplation of the works of ECK.

Paul Twitchell specifies in *The Spiritual Notebook* that "The ECK Masters did not reach their high state by fleeing from pain, or from finding comfort or sensual pleasures." The ECK Masters are hard workers in the physical body. Those ECKists who are sincere about their spiritual unfoldment will discipline themselves with the Friday fasts.

Those beings who work in the Temples of Golden Wisdom, both on the physical plane and beyond, receive their instructions from the spiritual hierarchy and quietly carry out their duties as effectively as possible. Their demeanor is uplifting and cheerful. And why not? After all, they are Co-workers with God!

A Higher Initiate from Africa was presented with the question: "What would you do to present the message of ECK if you suddenly moved to the United States?" At first he tactfully reserved an answer, but after careful reflection, he replied, "To do it effectively, the initiates of ECK must learn to work together. There must also be frequent HU Chants." Those areas that practice this are generally leaders in reaching the uninitiated.

When we work together to accomplish whatever goals we set for ourselves, there is created a vortex for Spirit to work in. Our individual efforts are magnified many times so that the greatest goals are achieved with greater ease.

The ECKist who quietly puts out the ECK message in some way is working for his own spiritual unfoldment.

There is a lot to be said about what one gains from serving the ECK. In short, when one gives without ever thinking of rewards, he is in the first stage of immortality.

Charles Kuralt wrote of one exceptional character who tired of arguing for a project he believed in, so he started to build the highway himself!

35

How to Become an ECK Master

Here are clues for you on how to develop into ECK Mastership. Somebody claimed that the only creature on earth free from boredom is a dog. I should like to include ECKists as well.

An ECK Master is never bored, no matter what he does or where he goes. A few years ago an article by Charles Kuralt appeared in *Family Circle* magazine. It studied classic attitudes of exceptional characters who, although unaware of the teachings of ECK, certainly practiced the life of ECK.

All of Kuralt's exceptional characters were people of action, even as you will find in your study of the ECK Masters: In some way, they serve life.

"The world is sustained by every action whose sole object is sacrifice," observed Yaubl Sacabi. "That is, the voluntary gift of self."

A Minnesota man in his midfifties, tired of arguing for his pet project of a *straight* highway between Duluth, Minnesota, and Fargo, North Dakota, stopped talking and started doing. Wheeling out a sturdy wheelbarrow, he got a shovel and a relic of a John Deere

219

tractor. He resolved to build the road himself—an impossible span of two hundred miles.

A quarter of a century later, at the grand age of eighty-one, the robust fellow had completed eleven miles and continued ever strong toward his goal.

Nor was he a fool. Common sense suggested that a direct highway would prove to be a commercial boon to both Minnesota and North Dakota. The eleven paved miles, he hoped, would inspire state legislators to authorize funds to finish the visionary project. And so he worked on alone to fulfill his goal.

An ECK Master will urge the initiate to acquire and live by the highest attributes of total spiritual freedom, total awareness, and self-responsibility.

Myths linger from ancient religions of the Atlanteans and the Hittites. Priests then had already created a Divine Being both vengeful and good. Wrenching people's emotions back and forth between fear and love, they beat down the faith and spirit of man. Broken in will, man meekly accepted outer authority and the chains of spiritual bondage.

Today, mankind still yearns for a gracious, grandfatherly God who restores health and gives daily bread just because somebody asks. Where is self-responsibility?

God, however, is scarcely touched by the tears of creatures in the lower worlds. This fact shocks the orthodox mind. The SUGMAD actually administers the worlds through the Mahanta, the Living ECK Master. The Master himself, in the physical body, trusts totally in the ECK Power to reach all Souls ready to become one with the Essence of God, the ECK.

How does a chela with a serious problem get help? When anyone calls upon the Mahanta, the Living ECK Master, the problem may stay, but the inquirer gets a better understanding of it. The initiate goes within himself to find a better way to cope with life's changes, loss, or disappointment.

All is given in keeping with one's karma and spiritual development.

Total awareness, an attribute of the ECK Masters, means seeing things as a whole. This becomes a feature of the ECKist's attitude, for now he faces every problem in life, finding solutions without having to depend upon anyone else.

The ECK Masters immerse themselves in living. *The Shariyat-Ki-Sugmad* assures us that the the call of God may be other than serving in a monastery or sacred temple. A business career or motherhood can be the sphere that perfects the individual who heeds the call of Soul. How can we be of most service to other people?

So far, we have seen that to become an ECK Master takes courage, resourcefulness, and a desire to serve all life.

Another man Kuralt met was a professor of English in Ohio. The college administration pressured him into retirement at the age of seventy. The professor held to the ideals of work and dignity, wishing to contribute to the community as a productive citizen.

As soon as he had tendered his teaching resignation to the school officials, he hustled over to the gym and applied for a job as janitor. In his mind, productive work was essential for survival. Teaching English in the classroom had imparted many lessons, but so did cleaning up locker rooms.

Students eventually understood his need to grow and learn. Fifteen years later, at the age of eighty-five, this youthful spirit still left his surroundings better than he had found them.

<u>Commit yourself to the ECKshar and to God Consciousness.</u> An excuse that twenty minutes a day is too much time to spend on the Spiritual Exercises of ECK shows little self-discipline. This is like the fellow who talks of becoming a writer but gives all sorts of reasons why he does not write. The truth is, he simply is not committed to writing. Is the chela committed to the expansion of consciousness?

A gentleman from Tennessee brought home a startling insight from a Light and Sound Workshop in Nashville. The ECK leader made a statement on this order: "The Light and Sound are the keys to Self- and God-Realization. What are you willing to give up for them?"

The correspondent wrote, "I must say that this floored me. For a long time I have fooled myself to believe that everything would be handed to me on a silver platter. I suddenly realized that even if I'm shown the way, in the end I must do it myself!"

Three things needed for Soul's release from the wheel of karma and reincarnation are the Living ECK Master, the true initiation, and the Audible Life Current.

 More of the initiate's time is given over to contemplation, being himself, and service to the ECK. He strives for happiness through self-discipline. Whoever learns to yield to the pressures of life will survive both here and in the Far Country, the residence of the Order of Vairagi.

Your key to self-mastery is in this article.

The boy bowed before the fire that illuminated the jungle cave, and began to pray to the gods of the natives.

36

The Secret Doctrine

The secret doctrine is the portion of the Shariyat-Ki-Sugmad that the Mahanta passes to the chela by means of the Spiritual Exercises of ECK. This is the only authentic road to God, the one all spiritual travelers take to Mastership.

While Peddar Zaskq, known to us as Paul Twitchell, was directing me through the disciplines of ECK, he wanted to get across the concept of God-Realization. He did this once through an illustrative cartoon from *The Phantom* series that I recall from the Sunday comics I read as a boy.

The Phantom was a jungle hero dressed in a striking violet uniform. Always masked, he preserved law and order in the forests, prevailing against the dark forces that invaded his territory. He came from a long line of past Phantoms who had for centuries been the protectors of the helpless natives in the jungle. His lineage was much like that of the Order of the Vairagi ECK Adepts.

Peddar Zaskq had lifted me in the Soul body to the Causal Plane, above the fabled Time Track. A scene unfolded around the selection and training of a young lad, who was picked from among a number of other boys and painstakingly trained to become the next Phantom. Little by little his future assignments were shown to him by his ever-present teacher.

One day the boy bowed himself in the dirt before a fire that illuminated the deep jungle cave. Here he began to pray to the gods of the natives, as he had seen them do since his childhood. Immediately, his teacher stepped from the shadows and chided him, "Why do you pray?"

The youth made no answer, for he was imitating the natives, who were animists.

"You must know that no gods, no invisible spirits, exist except you. You are like God! Why pray to an invisible God?"

Peddar Zaskq explained the impossibility of one ever becoming God. But the individual could someday put on the cloak of God Consciousness, which is being the ECK.

The point here was that the old, orthodox concept of God had to be dislodged from my head before the love of the SUGMAD could enter into my heart. This old image of God had been a corruption from the ancient pages of the Shariyat, and was a detriment to the child of ECK.

The Mahanta meets us inwardly in a wide variety of settings. They are places for him to impart the teaching that would be rejected out of hand if given in a way that clashed with our built-in sense of propriety, of what is right.

Therefore, the secret doctrine is aligned with our present education until we can grow into the greater vision of truth. One time I traveled to a lecture on the inner planes where Paul Twitchell was speaking to a crowd about Saint Paul, the apostle. He was relating the apostle's life to the audience in terms of the spiritual

226

significance that governed this man's actions. All the while he kept a piercing gaze fastened upon me in the audience, which made me squirm with discomfort. His eyes then became faraway and distant during the remainder of the lecture. When he had finished the talk, he again caught my eye and asked by the clear voice of telepathy, "Will you return to learn more?" It seemed there was more to teach, as indeed there was. Many times did he come to give encouragement to my quest for the supreme consciousness, yet he never forced the teachings of ECK upon me in any way.

One day Paul came during contemplation to tell me to move to another part of the western United States. This sort of news usually upset me, because I was a person who treasured familiar surroundings. I had been living in Las Vegas in the early seventies, and Paul said that I would soon go to the West Coast, perhaps south of Los Angeles. This move seemed highly unlikely then, but as time proved out it did come about as he had predicted on the inner planes.

Paul at this point had been around so long in my inner worlds that I confess to having taken him for granted at times, as did a lot of chelas then. But the wave of love flowing from his eyes into mine left little doubt as to the nature of the Mahanta of the age.

A glint in his eyes hinted at the future. "I believe we'll take you to Los Angeles and look for a job," he said. "The ECK-Vidya will open up if we go there."

A sharp reluctance arose in me. I was home and comfortable, so why go off looking for trouble? I suggested, "We don't have to drive all that way! I can probably get the ECK-Vidya tonight at bedtime."

But Paul insisted good-naturedly to go there anyway. "It'll be pork and beans," he said, hinting that good food would be scarce for a while.

"Oh, that's all right," I replied too quickly. "I like pork and beans." Six months later I was to regret this eagerness, because several weeks went by where I was without a job, and indeed there was very little to eat but pork and beans with bread. The change was to expose me to a side of life that would later help in my present duties as the spiritual head of ECKANKAR; therefore, hardship or not, I went.

The secret doctrine is more than an imagined, dull recitation of words from an old book in a remote temple. The Mahanta, the Living ECK Master gives a chela actual experience on the spiritual planes. This method of operation is a puzzle to the orthodox mind, which has been accustomed to enduring hollow sermons from the pulpit. Nevertheless, it is the only way I know to get a pure insight into the creation of God.

Another night I practiced the spiritual exercises and found myself traveling through the created journey of time and space. While seated in contemplation, I rocked back and forth like a clock's pendulum. Suddenly, I slipped into the Soul body and began to move swiftly on the inner planes. Fear had paralyzed me until I finally let go of it and crashed through a binding wall, moving backward down an endless corridor of ancient pillars while the sound of ECK, like a whistling roar of a jet engine, rushed past my ears.

As this experience progressed, I noted that strong magnetic waves of light emanated from me as Soul while I sang a secret name for God. Ripples of Sound flowed outward to throw up an invincible shield that protected my journey. I was Soul and was seeing my state of consciousness accept lightning-fast changes around itself in the form of travel through time and space. This was an excursion into the worlds of being, and thus there never really was travel anywhere—

because Soul dwells always in the present moment, collapsing the illusion of time and space.

In the Soul body I had left the bedroom and had swept out from the physical universes, leaving them far behind. I knew myself as Soul—timeless—and the world as small, petty, and insignificant. It was significant only if I chose to favor it with conscious reflection, and that decision would put me exactly in the center of it.

Meanwhile, I participated consciously in a region far beyond the mundane physical firmament in both time and space. Far removed, yet as close as my heartbeat. This is a difficult thing to describe, so you must do your best to learn the formulas of ECK and see for yourself.

Wah Z means the secret doctrine. The Shariyat is taught in free verse, narrative, legends, or stories. As Paul said of it in the introduction to *The Shariyat-Ki-Sugmad,* Book One: "Sometimes it is in allegories or fables. But altogether it is the whole truth, concise in all its parts and tells everyone what life really consists of and how to live it."

Before you leave this life, take the trouble to learn the secret doctine of ECK. It is the Law of Love which alone can carry you to God.

The physical plane is designed as a good place to earn
ECK Mastership. It is a fast school for learning.

37

Journey to God-Realization

There is an awakening occurring among the initiates of ECK that it really is possible to reach Self-Realization and God-Realization, and to realize the Kingdom of Heaven while still living in the body.

When we stop unfolding, it is simply because we have forgotten the spiritual goals set before us when we initially stepped upon the path of ECK. One of the first was to get the linkup with the ECK Sound Current. After that took place, some of us did not care too much what happened next. No more reincarnations on earth; the struggle seemed won. This marked the Second Initiation.

Others did overcome self-satisfaction long enough to resume the disciplines that had borne them this far. They now set their aim toward reaching the Soul Plane and becoming established there.

Enthusiasm and love for the ECK carried us from the time we stepped upon the path, through the Second Initiation. We attended ECK introductory lectures, gave out books, practiced the spiritual exercises, studied the ECK discourses. We lived the life of ECK with true devotion, seeing moment to moment what Divine Spirit brought into our lives for spiritual upliftment. Somewhere along the line, however, the negative influences dampened our enthusiasm.

A letter from an ECKist reflects this concern. He writes, "It has been my understanding from studying the teachings of ECK that after the Second Initiation, the individual would not have to return to another incarnation unless he or she chose to do so."

He reported a dream that suggested he would have to return for another incarnation whether he wanted this or not. Quite emphatically he stated that if he had his way, he would not come back to another physical incarnation. Rather, he wanted to continue his development toward ECK Mastership, if he did not reach it in this lifetime.

The physical plane is designed as a good place to earn ECK Mastership, although it can be done on any number of planes. It is a fast school for learning.

Whether or not Rebazar Tarzs resides in his hut, a lowly shelter on the physical plane, he has direct contact with the SUGMAD anytime he chooses, no matter where he is stationed as a Co-worker with God.

Realizing that we must continue to work for our unfoldment beyond the Second Initiation, we can release our attachment to the idea of never returning to the physical plane. We then begin working earnestly for spiritual liberation in this lifetime.

The attitude of dreading a return to the physical body holds us back from spiritual unfoldment.

Another letter from an ECKist says that "I was rereading one of the earlier *Wisdom Notes* by Paul Twitchell, and he was reminding us to pay attention to all these small duties in this life. For you never know how they may lead you along the path to the SUGMAD."

Whenever a person came to Paul with a problem, he tried to get the individual, in some way, to act upon the problem himself, rather than depending on Paul for a solution. As the Mahanta, the Living ECK Master, he wanted the individual Souls under his care to someday become Masters in their own right. How could they become ECK Masters if he did all their thinking for them? He tried to point out that the solution for every problem is available within us.

There is a resting point that occurs for many people after the Second Initiation. They feel they have made it. They'll sit there and look around for a couple of months, or perhaps a couple of years, before the gentle nudging of the ECK comes through that there is another heaven to go. Don't stop, go on.

A number of the ECK initiates are aware of the current opportunity to develop as a greater vehicle for Spirit. The following letter attests to that: "I and many, many ECKists are aware of a tremendous surge of energy since the spiritual new year commenced. With this surge comes a knowingness that it provides an opportunity for us to tune in to this energy and serve as greater vehicles than before."

Diligently, one reviews the disciplines that brought him to his present point on the spiritual path, picking up on the four fundamentals of ECKANKAR. The first is self-discipline. Then, the absolute inner reliance on the Mahanta. Third, the Spiritual Exercises of ECK. And, finally, the true contemplation of the works of ECK.

Now Soul again begins the journey through the lower worlds toward Its original goal of Self-Realization on the Soul Plane.

A curious thing sometimes happens once the individual reaches the Soul Plane. It is almost a study in history of what happened back when he got the Second Initiation. He takes a rest! He hardly believes that he can make God-Realization. The feeling is: "Hey, I've made it this far. Let's not rock the boat."

Paul Twitchell pointed this out in *The Wisdom Notes* of December 1968, and he said: "It is imperative that the initiates never stop on the way to reach membership within the true order of the ECK Masters. To do so is spiritual death and this brings [them] to a complete halt in any advancement to the God arena."

The initiates are realizing, often for the first time, that it is possible to reach their former goals. Not everyone will make it, because not everyone will apply himself to the disciplines.

The path becomes more subtle. There shines a sweet humility as the candidate for ECK Adept reaches into the higher God Worlds of ECK.

We must work for our own spiritual unfoldment. There will be no cheerleaders applauding on the sidelines. Hardly anyone will be aware of our experiences in the Sound and Light of ECK as we obey the Law of Silence. The inner initiations may come years before the pink slip that invites us to complete the cycle of the initiation on the physical plane.

We become a Co-worker with God at every step of the spiritual path. That is a universal law. There is great hope here for those who are sincere in finding out who and what they are, becoming a Co-worker with God, and realizing the Kingdom of Heaven while still living in the body. The key lies within you.

The Living ECK Master can assist, show the way, but each individual must walk the steps himself.

Because the little boy could not see how close his feet were to the floor, he was afraid and was repeating, "Help me, God! Help me, God!" over and over.

38

A Wonderland of Love

If God wants ye for anything, there is nothing ye can do about it. He will draw ye unto Him in some manner or other without ye ever realizing it. Through the heart of a woman, or a child, it matters not to Him. (Rebazar Tarzs speaks to Peddar Zaskq in *Stranger by the River.*)

A child of three had gotten himself into a predicament. He was lying on his stomach across two chairs, his feet dangling above the floor. Unable to see the floor beneath him, he was afraid to let go and slide the few inches to safety.

The father, who observed his son fussing on the chair, at first thought it was because the boy had gotten stuck. Then he realized what the child was saying. He was repeating, "Help me, God! Help me, God!" over and over. The father couldn't help but laugh. His son's obstacle, so easy for the father, seemed worthy of divine intervention to the boy.

But then the father considered how often he too had bewailed his own situation, too scared to let go. How often did people plead for divine intervention to chase away some fleeting obstacle instead of learning the lesson? The father's love for his son had allowed him to recognize himself. And yet, the Mahanta is always present, to bestow love and protection upon all who love him.

In ECK, contemplation brings the God seeker to a wonderland of love. It is a new creation, a new state of consciousness. The golden key to this wonderful place inside each person is the act of surrender.

Right before an ECK seminar, an ECK student accidentally got carbon monoxide poisoning. At a restaurant, during the seminar, she was further a victim of food poisoning. The combination of one poison upon the other made her very ill. Later at home, facing a demanding schedule at school, she went into contemplation to ask the Mahanta how to maintain balance and remain a clear channel for ECK.

The Master took her to a room in a Temple of Golden Wisdom. It was a dark, nondescript room with a podium. A column of shimmering white light, with a sensation of motion in it, shone upon the podium. She was told to place her right hand upon it, and as she did, the right side of her body began to gently, then strongly, vibrate with a vitalizing life-force. In comparison, her left side felt dead.

As she wondered at that, the Master laughed and suggested that she also touch the podium with her left hand. Then that hand began to fill with the wonderful vitalizing force. She noticed that the air she was breathing in the chamber was cool, like air on a mountaintop.

As she continued to breathe deeply, she felt her Spiritual Eye open, and the ECK flowed in and out of her. This continued until both sides of her had reached an equilibrium—a harmony in vibration, a balance that seemed to spiral between the two sides. Then as she turned toward the Mahanta, he said, "You might not feel like eating much for a while." As she was leaving the temple, he added that she could return whenever necessary.

The Master was right: Food did not agree with her for a few days. Since then, whenever she feels she is overextending herself to reach goals she has set in the physical, she returns to that special temple to regain her equilibrium. She considers it a privilege to use, not abuse.

This wonderland of love first reaches into the individual but then reaches out to the world in service. A woman and her husband were to meet another ECK couple in a train station. While waiting for them in the restaurant, they struck up a conversation with a stranger, whose wife had died a number of years ago. Since that time he had been without love in his life.

The couple listened to his story. After the man had told it, he asked them, "Who are you that you would bother to listen to me?"

The ECKists could see how obvious it was that the ECK wanted to comfort him. When they parted, the man's face was radiant and happy, perhaps for the first time in years.

The couple had been enroute to an ECK seminar. At the Sunday morning HU Chant, the wife fell asleep. Because of the love she had shown to the stranger in the train station, the Mahanta took her via Soul Travel to a certain point in the inner worlds where there was a sort of primary beginning: the creation of the lower worlds. Creation was yet very simple.

It was from this central point that everything started, and she heard these wonderful words: "Since the beginning of all time."

She was being shown that before and after creation, the HU had always been there. It was her special seminar experience.

Two days after the seminar, this ECK initiate was alone in the home of her parents, who were now deceased. She was to clean out and sort a pile of boxes and bags. In them she discovered many pieces of clothing she had worn as a child. Her mother had kept these items because she loved her daughter. As each box was opened, an enormous treasure of love flowed from it. It was love without beginning or end—like the HU. Sorting through these old things and feeling the love in them gave her a deep reverence for her mother's love—and for Divine Love as well.

She realized that when personal love opens the door to Divine Love, none of the problems and trials of karma are in vain. What had nourished her through every day of every lifetime was Divine Love. Nothing could exist without it. It was the reason she existed. When there was no resistance on her part, when old ideas and old patterns were emptied from her, then she would always know that Divine Love was her reason for living. In it, she would always dwell.

 The wonderland of ECK is the universe of Sound and Light. It is all those places where creation thrives. Where the spiritual travelers go to explore the glory of Divine Love.

An initiate in Africa read a lesson of the *Soul Travel 1* discourses. After doing the spiritual exercise in the lesson, he shut his eyes to sleep. Far off in the distance he saw a dot of golden light: dim at first, it then began to move rapidly toward him. It grew in size until it was revealed as the ⊕ symbol—the letters EK. Its color was that of an old bronze metal with a good many dents on the polished surface. This was to demonstrate the enduring nature of ECK.

A simple spiritual exercise is this: At bedtime, concentrate upon the golden letters ᛟ and softly chant HU, the sacred name of God. Soon you should see the Light and hear the Sound of God.

The exercise is your key to the wonderland of God's Divine Love.

Glossary of ECKANKAR Terms

Words set in SMALL CAPS are defined elsewhere in the Glossary

ARAHATA. An experienced and qualified teacher for ECKANKAR classes.

CHELA. A spiritual student.

ECK. The Life Force, the Holy Spirit, or Audible Life Current which sustains all life.

ECKANKAR. The Ancient Science of SOUL TRAVEL. A truly spiritual religion for the individual in modern times, known as the secret path to God via dreams and Soul Travel. The teachings provide a framework for anyone to explore their own spiritual experiences. Established by Paul Twitchell, the modern-day founder, in 1965.

ECK MASTERS. Spiritual Masters who can assist and protect people in their spiritual studies and travels. The ECK Masters are from a long line of God-Realized Souls who know the responsibility that goes with spiritual freedom.

HU. The secret name for God. The singing of the word HU, pronounced like the man's name Hugh, is considered a love song to God. It is sung in the ECK Worship Service.

INITIATION. Earned by the ECK member through spiritual unfoldment and service to God. The initiation is a private ceremony in which the individual is linked to the Sound and Light of God.

LIVING ECK MASTER. The title of the spiritual leader of ECKANKAR. His duty is to lead Souls back to God. The Living ECK Master can assist spiritual students physically as the Outer Master, in the dream state as the Dream Master, and in

243

the spiritual worlds as the Inner Master. Sri Harold Klemp became the Living ECK Master in 1981.

MAHANTA. A title to describe the highest state of God Consciousness on earth, often embodied in the LIVING ECK MASTER. He is the Living Word.

PLANES. The levels of heaven, such as the Astral, Causal, Mental, Etheric, and Soul planes.

SATSANG. A class in which students of ECK study a monthly lesson from ECKANKAR.

THE SHARIYAT-KI-SUGMAD. The sacred scriptures of ECKANKAR. The scriptures are comprised of twelve volumes in the spiritual worlds. The first two were transcribed from the inner planes by Paul Twitchell, modern-day founder of ECKANKAR.

SOUL. The True Self. The inner, most sacred part of each person. Soul exists before birth and lives on after the death of the physical body. As a spark of God, Soul can see, know, and perceive all things. It is the creative center of Its own world.

SOUL TRAVEL. The expansion of consciousness. The ability of Soul to transcend the physical body and travel into the spiritual worlds of God. Soul Travel is taught only by the Living ECK Master. It helps people unfold spiritually and can provide proof of the existence of God and life after death.

SOUND AND LIGHT OF ECK. The Holy Spirit. The two aspects through which God appears in the lower worlds. People can experience them by looking and listening within themselves and through Soul Travel.

SPIRITUAL EXERCISES OF ECK. The daily practice of certain techniques to get us in touch with the Light and Sound of God.

SUGMAD. A sacred name for God. SUGMAD is neither masculine nor feminine; IT is the source of all life.

WAH Z. The spiritual name of Sri Harold Klemp. It means the Secret Doctrine. It is his name in the spiritual worlds.

Bibliography

"The Carriers of Truth." *The Mystic World*, September–October 1982.

"ECKANKAR: The New-Age Religion." *The Mystic World*, Winter 1987.

"The Eye of the Tiger." *The Mystic World*, Spring 1985.

"The Golden Heart." *The Mystic World*, Winter 1985.

"The Hidden Treasure." *The ECK Mata Journal*, 1983.

"How to Become an ECK Master." *The Mystic World*, Summer 1983.

"How to Keep a Dream Book." *The Mystic World*, Summer 1988.

"The Illuminated State." *The ECK Mata Journal*, 1987.

"In Search of God." *The Mystic World*, Summer 1986.

"It's All in the Game." *The Mystic World*, Fall 1988.

"The Journey to God-Realization." *The Mystic World*, March–April 1982.

"The Law of Gratitude." *The Mystic World*, Fall 1987.

"The Living Word." *The Mystic World*, Spring 1986.

"The Mahanta and Soul Travel." *The Mystic World*, Summer 1985.

"Methods of the Black Magician." *The Mystic World*, Winter 1983.

"The Odyssey of Soul." *The Mystic World*, Fall 1986.

"Paul Twitchell: The Writer." *The Mystic World*, Summer 1984.

"Prince or Pauper?" *The Mystic World*, Spring 1988.

"The Razor's Edge." *The Mystic World,* Fall 1985.

"The Sacred Dreamer." *The Mystic World,* January–February 1983.

"The Secret Doctrine." *The Mystic World,* Fall 1984.

"The Seed of Fortune." *The Mystic World,* Spring 1987.

"The Shadow of Truth." *The Mystic World,* Spring 1983.

"The Soft Kiss of God." *The ECK Mata Journal,* 1985.

"Soul Travel Today." *The Mystic World,* Winter 1986.

"The Sound and Light of Heaven." *The ECK Mata Journal,* 1987.

"The Spiritual Crib." *The Mystic World,* November–December 1982.

"'Stop the World I Want to Get Off'... *or* When Will You Leave ECK?" *The Mystic World,* Winter 1984.

"Storms of Trial." *The Mystic World,* Spring 1984.

"The Way of the ECK-Vidya." *The Mystic World,* May–June 1982.

"What Is Truth?" *The Mystic World,* Fall 1983.

"What Really Is the Word of God?" *The ECK Mata Journal,* 1988.

"What the Old Religions Forgot." *The ECK Mata Journal,* 1986.

"When Discipline Goes Wrong." *The Mystic World,* Summer 1987.

"When Religion Fails Her Children." *The ECK Mata Journal,* 1984.

"A Wonderland of Love." *The Mystic World,* Winter 1988.

"A Word or Two on Drugs." *The Mystic World,* July–August 1982.

"Working Together in ECK." *The Mystic World,* January–February 1982.

Index

247

248

Chant(ing)
AUM, 11
HU. *See* HU
Mahanta, 164
secret word. *See* Word(s): secret
SUGMAD, 148
Charlemagne, 167–69
Chastity, 82
Chela(s). *See also* ECKist(s)
experiences of, 155, 215
and Inner Master. *See* Inner Master: and chela
and karma, 98
and Living ECK Master. *See* Living ECK Master: and chela
and past Masters, 1, 2, 3
and personality of Master, 2, 110, 131
and Paul Twitchell. *See* Twitchell, Paul: and chelas
prepared for inner experience, 138
with serious problems, 220–21
and sincere Christians, 77
and spiritual exercises, 51
Child(ren). *See also* Youth
of ECK, 226
experiences of, 30, 237
Christian(ity), 18. *See also* Bible, Jesus Christ; Saint(s)
believers in, 50, 63
born-again, 192
communities, 87
early, 4, 5, 69, 85
ECKists and, 77, 192
and Light and Sound, 20
Chuba, 1, 2, 5
Church(es). *See also* Christian(ity); Religion(s), religious
Catholic, 63, 75, 85, 86
clergy, 69, 76. *See also* Priest(s), priestcraft

councils, 5
doctrine. *See* Doctrine(s): church
orthodox. *See* Orthodox religion(s)
services, 4, 26
Cleansing, 5, 206
Cliff Hanger, 99, 100, 106
Color(s), 28, 146
Columbus, Christopher, 164
Comfort, 104, 239
Comforter. *See* ECK; Holy Spirit
Common sense, 155, 220
Communication, 2, 35, 37. *See also* Talk(ing); Write, writer(s), writing
Communion, 20, 33, 54. *See also* Church(es): services
Community work, 95
Compassion, 45, 82, 104, 127
Competitiveness, 189
Complication, 197
Confession, 33
Confidence, 120
Confirmation, 36, 54
Consciousness
animal, 125
changes in, 80, 161, 183, 206, 210, 228
Christ, 164
cosmic, 80
ECKshar. *See* ECKshar
gift of, 175, 176
God. *See* God: Consciousness
high(er) states of, 44, 75, 81, 116, 169, 215
human, 4, 12, 22, 61, 62, 75, 104, 119, 145, 147, 149, 164, 169, 182, 204, 205
level(s) of, 20, 22, 25, 95, 146, 238
Mahanta. *See* Mahanta: Consciousness
opens, 120
pure, 42
social, 22, 139, 200, 203, 204
spiritual, 33, 53, 203

Disease. *See* Illness(es)
Doctor(s), 125, 128
Doctrine(s)
  church, 5, 49, 69, 85, 86
  of ECKANKAR, 22, 74, 75,
    76, 117, 140
  empty, 58
  secret, 225, 226, 228, 229
Dog, 219
Dogma, 57, 74, 76, 77
Doubt(s), 70, 109, 110
  avoiding, 120
Dream(s), dream state
  book, 113, 114–15, 117
  changes in, 111
  and ECK Masters, 33
  and ECK-Vidya, 155, 162
  experience(s) in, 30, 115,
    119, 120, 121, 149
  fear motif in, 121, 133
  images, 114, 115–16
  interpreting, 115, 147, 194,
    232
  invasion of, 133
  journal. *See* Dream(s),
    dream state: book
  Mahanta and, 13, 115, 119,
    138
  as phase in ECKANKAR,
    145, 146
  realizing a. *See* Goal(s)
  recall, 111, 116
  recurring, 34
  research, 113
  study of, 114
Drugs, 10, 125–28
Dumas, Alexandre, 197
Duty, duties, 131, 232

Eagle, 1
Earth, 18, 44, 55, 67, 85, 140,
  149, 160, 163, 181, 193,
  219, 231
Easy Way, the. *See* Tech-
  nique(s): the Easy Way
Eating, 239
ECK
  aspects of the, 44, 149, *See*

also Light and Sound
  becoming one with, 25, 165,
    197, 200, 226
  bringing spiritual revolu-
    tion, 95
  call on, 121, 193–94
  and chela, 127, 211
  embodiment of the, 42, 141.
    See also Mahanta
  enduring nature of, 241
  as Essence of God, 69, 220
  expression of, 2
  four fundamentals of,
    215–16, 233
  Gospel of, 212
  help from, 187, 220
  holy fire of. *See* Holy: fire of
    ECK
  how, works, 41
  initiates. *See* Initiate(s)
  Lady of. *See* Simha, the Lady
    of ECK
  leads Soul to God, 46
  manifestations of, 28
  Marg, 75
  message of, 34, 122, 132,
    211, 216
  path of, 14, 27, 70, 76, 85,
    109, 127, 128, 198, 231
  Power, 26, 186, 220
  talking about, 10, 193
  understanding of, 147
ECKANKAR
  Ancient Science of Soul
    Travel, 161
  arguments about, 77
  authenticity of, 68
  birth of, 83, 93
  books, 14, 51, 82, 155, 211,
    212, 231. *See also*
    ECKANKAR — The Key to
    Secret Worlds; Flute of
    God, The; In My Soul I Am
    Free; Shariyat-Ki-
    Sugmad, The; Shariyat-
    Ki-Sugmad, The, Book
    One; *Shariyat-Ki-*
    Sugmad, The; Book Two;

251

ECKANKAR *(continued)*
  Spiritual Notebook, The;
  Stranger by the River;
  Tiger's Fang, The
  building program in, 82
  churches and, 63
  discourses, 82, 120, 142, 155,
    231. *See also ECK Dream*
    Discourses, The; Soul
    Travel 1—The Illumi-
    nated Way
  early years of, 109
  experiences prior to, 43, 51
  experiences in, 12, 149
  finding, 27, 42, 45, 49, 210
  future of, 83
  introducing others to, 122,
    212
  leaving, 101
  life of, 231
  membership of, 154, 205
  mission of. *See* Mission: of
    ECKANKAR
  new students of, 11, 13–14,
    146
  Office, 187
  opposition to, 22, 69, 87
  path of, 38, 79, 80, 154
  Paul Twitchell and. *See*
    Twitchell, Paul: as
    Mahanta
  purpose of, 23, 75, 126
  and religious freedom, 89
  Satsang classes, 50
  seminar(s), 43, 121, 163,
    169, 175, 176, 205,
    210–11, 222, 238, 239
  spiritual new year for, 215,
    233
  study of, 119, 156, 175, 185
  teachings, 11, 56, 62, 67, 74,
    76, 79, 132, 140, 219
ECKANKAR—The Key to
  Secret Worlds, 46, 86, 137,
  138
ECK Dream Discourses, The,
  46
ECKist(s)

being used by Spirit. *See*
  Spirit: being used by
is never bored, 219
experiences of, 34, 38, 69,
  146, 192, 215, 239
and initiations, 121, 232
loves life, 210
Mahanta and, 115, 120
mission of, 25, 211
is not a mystic, 30
persecution of, 22
spiritual life of, 122, 160, 216
ECK Master(s), 33, 36, 199.
  See also Fubbi Quantz;
  Gopal Das; Kai-Kuas;
  Ketu Jaraul; Lai Tsi;
  Living ECK Master;
  Mahanta; Peddar Zaskq;
  Pythagoras; Rama;
  Rebazar Tarzs; Simha,
  the Lady of ECK;
  Tamaqui; Tomo Geshig;
  Twitchell, Paul; Vairagi,
  Order of; Wah Z; Yaubl
  Sacabi; Zadok
  attributes of, 221
  are never bored, 219
  and chela, 111, 122, 220. *See*
    also Disciple(s): of ECK
    Master
  and death. *See* Death: of Kai-
    Kuas
  and ECK-Vidya readings,
    153
  existence of, 67, 69–70
  love of, 209
  meeting with, 34, 69, 122
  and rise to Mastership, 2,
    216, 233
  in Silver Age, 164
  and study of spiritual con-
    sciousness, 53
ECKshar, 80, 145, 149, 161,
  222
ECK-Vidya, 153–56, 167–68,
  169, 171, 176, 177, 227
  readings, 153, 156
Economy, 13. *See also* Law(s):

of Economy
Education, 9, 68, 160. *See also*
    Teacher(s), teaching(s)
  religious, 22, 55
  of Soul, 198, 232
Ego, 97
  conflict with, 189
ᛋ symbol, 240–41
Emotions, emotional, 107, 220
  body. *See* Body(ies): Astral
    (emotional)
  freedom from, 156
  Plane. *See* Plane(s): Astral
  study of, 161
  tricks, 134
Enlightenment, 13, 36, 92,
    106, 149
Envy, 181
Esau, 62
Eternity, 10, 162
Evangelist(s), 12
Evil, 81, 203
Exercises, spiritual. *See* Spiri-
    tual Exercises of ECK
Expectations, 187
Experience(s)
  dream. *See* Dream(s), dream
    state: experience(s) in
  in higher worlds, 33, 103,
    120
  inner. *See* Inner: experi-
    ence(s) with Light and
    Sound. *See* Light and
    Sound: experiences with
  lower world, 109
  phenomenal, 110
  at seminars, 240
  Soul Travel. *See* Soul Travel:
    experiences
  spiritual. *See* Spiritual: ex-
    periences
  subtle, 137
  teaches us, 192
  yardstick of, 97

Failure, 25, 186
  in duty to God, 131
  in ECK, 119

reasons for, 194
  of religion, 9, 14, 74, 76
Faith, 3, 54, 149, 220
  in ECK, 77
Fame, 93, 94, 139
Families, 154, 221. *See also*
    Child(ren)
  spiritual study in, 114
Family Circle magazine, 219
Far Country, 12, 117, 139, 163,
    188, 222
Fasting, 179, 216. *See also*
    Cleansing
Fate, 177
Fear(s), 9, 63, 204
  of death. *See* Death: fear of
  of error, 170
  experiences with, 37, 82,
    171, 237
  of others, 88
  and psychic forces, 132, 133
  in religion, 220
  getting rid of, 5, 27, 109, 120,
    174
  and Soul Travel, 11, 43, 228
Fights, 134
Finances, 115, 154. *See also*
    Money
Flute of God, The, 110, 186
Food. *See* Eating; Soul: food for
Forces
  dark, 135
  of nature, 170
  projector, 170
  psychic. *See* Psychic: forces
  tractor, 170
Fortune
  cookies, 177
  good, 185
  seed of, 175, 176
Freedom, 44, 83
  as attribute of God, 42
  ECK as path of, 14
  for individual, 85, 86, 126
  to leave ECK, 80
  religious, 86, 89
  search for, 163
  Soul's, 133

Freedom *(continued)*
    spiritual, 3, 33, 46, 98, 126,
        165, 197, 204–5, 215, 220
    of spiritual life, 185
French Revolution, 159
Freud, Sigmund 94, 161
Friendship, 193
Frugality, 82
Fubbi Quantz, 2, 4, 29, 82, 131,
        154
    and ECKANKAR, 22
Fulfillment, 197, 198
Future, 79, 153, 156, 180. *See*
        also ECK-Vidya; Prophecy
    events, 154, 155, 167
    unfoldment and, 173
    warnings about, 177

Galileo, 164
Garden(s), 167–68
    of Eden, 199
Gibran, Kahlil, 61
Gift, giving, 122, 163, 211, 212
    to God, 210
    from heart, 163
    of life, 187
    of love, 163
    of self, 219
    to Spirit, 211
Gnosticism, 69
Goal(s), 128, 146, 220
    common, 204
    of God-Realization, 12, 154
    reaching, 191, 216, 239
    self-made, 169
    of Soul, 147, 233
    spiritual, 119, 231
God
    agents of, 34, 58, 132
    aspects of, 35, 82. *See also*
        Light and Sound
    cannot become one with, 10,
        25, 226
    concepts about, 9, 53, 220,
        226
    Consciousness, 12, 26, 35,
        80, 103, 105, 145, 149, 162,
        199, 200, 204, 222, 226.

    See also God-Realization
    Co-worker with, 10, 25, 42,
        61, 97, 147, 182, 197, 211,
        215, 216, 232, 234
    duty to, 131, 205
    Essence of, 12, 69
    gift of, 109, 110
    heart of. *See* Heart: of God
    help from, 237
    journey to, 34, 42, 57, 128,
        132, 137, 145, 150, 197
    Kingdom of, 26, 28, 36, 37,
        41, 73, 141, 145, 180
    kiss of, 163
    love for, 35, 92, 104, 111
    name of, 35, 164, 169, 228,
        241. *See also* HU
    one, 76
    path to, 2, 77, 79, 180, 225.
        See also ECK: path of;
        SUGMAD: path to
    power of. *See* Power(s): of
        God
    princes of, 167
    search for, 54, 104, 110, 145,
        156
    secrets of, 34
    seeing, 131
    social, 203, 205
    and Soul, 61, 62, 80
    and study of religion, 56
    Voice of. *See* Voice of God
Godman, 3, 74, 76, 81, 99
    as origin of all religion, 75
    training for, 100
God-Realization, 13, 14, 25, 28,
        75, 103, 104, 106, 139, 145,
        154, 197, 222, 225, 231, 234
God World(s), 17, 28, 36, 50,
        53, 69, 81, 147, 149, 150,
        193, 234
Golden age, 23, 168, 181
Golden Rule, 20
Golden-tongued Wisdom, 168,
        176, 177
Golden Wisdom Temples. *See*
        Temple(s): of Golden Wis-
        dom

Gopal Das, 140
Gossip, 181
Grace, 162, 199
Gratitude, 185, 186, 187, 189
Greed, 98, 163
Growing, 173, 176, 210, 211.
    See also Spiritual: growth
Guidance, 77, 168. *See also*
    Mahanta: guidance of
Guilt, 183

Habit(s), 126, 161
Happiness, 44, 154, 177, 198,
    222, 239
    search for, 174
Harmony, 238
Hawaii, 133
Healer(s), healing. *See also*
    Doctor(s); Health
    churches and, 63
    ECK and, 104, 127
    Soul Travel for, 138
    spiritual exercises and, 27
Health, 13, 119, 154, 160, 204
    regaining, 127, 220
Heart
    attacks, 134
    center, 106
    of ECK teachings, 38, 76
    gift from, 163. *See also* Gift,
        giving: from heart
    of God, 27, 41, 42
    Golden, 104, 105, 106
    grateful, 185, 186
    love entering, 104, 226
    open, 186
    pure, 109, 110
Heaven(s)
    Christian, 2, 30
    experiences in, 163
    finding, 182, 189
    gateway to, 161
    of God, 115
    keys to, 33, 35, 36, 38, 182
    Kingdom of, 10, 12, 30, 50,
        63, 76, 128, 149, 231, 234
    levels of, 233
    negative traits follow us to,

    163
    state of, 64
    viewpoints about, 162
    Wind from, 63
Hell, 26, 127
Here and now, 156
Hesse, Hermann, 70
Hierarchy
    Kal Niranjan's, 22
    spiritual, 11, 91, 131, 149,
        216
Highway story, 219–20
Hinduism, 18, 25
History, 12, 93, 94
    books, 88
    of Soul's incarnations, 97
    of religions, 20, 86
Holy
    days, 4
    fire of ECK, 14, 62
Holy Spirit, 41, 62, 63, 97, 146,
        199. *See also* ECK
Honesty, 81, 155
Hope(s), 5
Horse, 173–74
Horus, 4
HU, 58, 240
    Chant, 175, 176, 216, 239
    chanting, 37, 134, 164, 241
    singing, 35, 57, 64, 169, 228
    song of, 171
    sound of, 57
Hubbard, L. Ron, 100
Human
    consciousness. *See* Con-
        sciousness: human
    ideals, 104
    love, 104
    nature, 87, 139, 180
    race, 73, 99
    senses, 142
Humility, 82, 234
Hyperboreans, 132
Hypnotism, 133, 161

Idea(s), 9, 186, 232, 240
Illness(es), 13, 127, 133, 160,
    197

257

138, 142
mission of, 30, 141
new, 110
past, 1, 3, 109, 132, 139,
    167
Paul Twitchell as. *See*
    Twitchell, Paul: as
    Mahanta
Rebazar Tarzs as. *See*
    Rebazar Tarzs: as
    Mahanta
and research, 41, 53
shaking hands with, 121
spiritual name of, 37. *See
    also* Wah Z
Living Waters, 46. *See also*
    ECK
Living Word, the, 1, 3, 4,
    106
Logic, 116
Loneliness, 25, 120, 197
Longfellow, Henry
    Wadsworth, 10, 94
Love
    contemplation and, 148
    detached, 81
    divine, 207, 240, 241
    for ECK, 231
    of ECK, 46, 80, 154
    of ECK Masters, 209
    experiencing, 45
    for God, 34, 35, 37
    as key to heaven, 38
    the HU as, 240
    human, 104, 240
    learning about, 117, 194
    for Mahanta. *See* Mahanta:
        love for
    message of, 6
    in religion, 220
    returns of, 177, 238
    and Soul, 61, 80
    as step on path, 197
    of SUGMAD. *See*
        SUGMAD: love for
    wonderland of, 238, 239, 241
Lust, 110, 125
    for power, 131

Madman, The, 61
Magician, black, 131–35
Mahanta. *See also* Inner
    Master; Wah Z
    as agent of spiritual power,
        181
    Blue Light of, 45, 175–76
    cares for his beloved ones, 80
    and chela, 30, 36, 44, 97, 101,
        128, 148, 154, 156, 180,
        209, 225
    coming of the, 181
    Consciousness, 140, 141
    as embodiment of the ECK,
        42, 141
    expression of, 2
    guidance of, 77, 177
    as head of Vairagi, 33
    help from, 37, 121, 126, 127,
        149, 163, 171, 183, 238
    inner link with, 142
    on inner planes, 105, 193
    inner reliance on, 216, 233
    as Living Word. *See* Living
        Word, the
    love for, 81
    love of, 5, 51
    meeting, 41, 119, 120, 122,
        137, 138, 207, 226
    name of, 37, 95
    Paul Twitchell as. *See*
        Twitchell, Paul: as
        Mahanta
    physical form of. *See* Living
        ECK Master
    presence of, 29, 106, 176, 238
    protection of, 37, 51, 127,
        238
    and religions, 82
    resisting, 44
    and Soul, 75, 138, 206
    and Soul Travel, 239
    surrender to, 5, 206
    titles for, 81
    unchanging, 110
    Wah Z as. *See* Wah Z
Mahanta Maharai, 141
Maharaji, 141

259

Mahdis. *See* Initiate(s) in ECK:
    Fifth
Mammon, 132
Marketing, 98
Martial arts, 134
Martyr(s), 85
Master(s)
    and chela, 98
    ECK. *See* ECK Master(s);
        Living ECK Master
    Inner. *See* Inner Master;
        Mahanta
    notions about, 101
    Outer. *See* Outer Master
    past, 1, 4. *See also* Living
        ECK Master: past
Mastership, 2, 225
    formula for, 180
    training for, 69, 100, 219,
        232
Matrix, 121
Maugham, Somerset, 203
May the blessings be, 35
Memory, 29. *See also* Plane(s):
    Causal
Mental
    body. *See* Body(ies): Mental
    pictures, 186, 187
    Plane. *See* Plane(s): Mental
    poison, 199
    teachings, 53
Mercy, 148, 162
Merton, Thomas, 29
Metaphysics, 91
Mind
    above the mind, 42, 182
    cleanliness of, 82, 109
    creative, 187
    dangers of drugs to, 125, 126
    keeping an open, 9
    limits of, 56, 68, 186
    orthodox, 220, 228
    reactions of, 161
    screen of. *See* Inner: screen
    social, 98
    and struggle, 26
    study of, 161
    and study of religion, 56

Miracle, 155
Mission, 55, 70
    of ECKANKAR, 137
    of ECK Master(s), 2, 22
    of Paul Twitchell. *See*
        Twitchell, Paul: mission of
    of Soul, 25
Missionaries, 85
Mistake(s), 170, 205
Money, 115, 131
    charging, 100, 210
    earning, 182, 209
    as wealth, 13, 119, 198, 203
Monastery, 167, 203, 221. *See
    also* Katsupari Monastery
Monotheism, 18
Morals, 82, 86
Mormon church, 45
Moses, 27–28
Mystic(ism), 29, 30

Napoleon, 159, 160, 162
Nature(s), 179
    of Christ, 5
    forces of. *See* Forces: of na-
        ture
    human. *See* Human: nature
    of Mahanta, 227
    of Soul, 33
Nazis, 87, 88, 159
Negative
    energy, 81
    power. *See* Power(s): nega-
        tive
Nestorius, 5
Nicodemus, 28
Nightmares, 133
Nirat, 28
Nuclear threat, 13
Nuri Sarup, 51

Observing, 109, 174
Obstacles, 28, 188. *See also*
    Problem(s)
Occult, 49. *See also* Black
    magic; Psychic: forces
    projection, 145
Ocean of Love and Mercy, 106,

Seeker(s) *(continued)*
  of supreme consciousness,
    227
  of truth. *See* Truth: seeker(s)
    of
Self-
  defense, 81
  destruction, 127
  discipline. *See* Discipline(s):
    self-
  knowledge, 162
  mastery, 183, 198, 222
  remembering, 109
  satisfaction, 231
  sufficiency, 183
  surrender, 120. *See also*
    Surrender
Self-Realization, 14, 28, 222,
  231
Serenity, 133
Sermon(s), 12, 26, 228
Service, 2, 154
  to ECK, 95, 206, 217, 222
  deeds of, 97
  to God, 42, 209
  to others, 74, 182, 206, 221,
    239
Seven Storey Mountain, The,
  29
Shabda Dhun, 103
Shakey's Pizza Parlor, 100
Shariyat-Ki-Sugmad, the, 53,
  76, 182, 225, 226, 229
Shariyat-Ki-Sugmad, The, 1,
  6, 25, 74, 75, 125, 142, 209,
  221
Shariyat-Ki-Sugmad, The,
  Book One, 41, 44, 73, 229
Shariyat-Ki-Sugmad, The,
  Book Two, 81
Silence, 132
  ECK Masters going into the,
    132
Silver Age, 164
Simha, the Lady of ECK, 45
Sin(s), 20, 161, 164, 205
Sleep, 114, 134
Soap boxes story, 98

Social, society, 86, 180
  consciousness. *See* Con-
    sciousness: social
  conventions, 21
  living outside of, 99
  mind, 98
Solution(s), 80, 83, 155, 170,
  182, 221. *See also* Prob-
    lem(s): solving
  good, 187
"Song of Myself," 205
Sorcery, 132. *See also* Black
  magic
Soul
  birthright of, 30
  body. *See* Body(ies): Soul
  call of, 142, 205
  Dark Night of, 29
  earning right to hear of
    ECK, 92
  experiences of, 44, 110, 177,
    179, 210
  food for, 58, 61, 128
  and God, 25, 49, 62, 221
  God-intoxicated, 1, 104
  home of, 37, 68
  identity of, 9, 10
  inexperienced, 101, 198, 199
  and Light and Sound, 37, 64
  and love, 182, 226
  maturity of, 67
  past lives of, 153
  Plane. *See* Plane(s): Soul
  purpose of, 61, 119, 122, 147,
    181
  qualities of, 62, 81, 149, 160,
    229
  records, 156
  as spark of God, 26, 42, 83,
    200
  survival of. *See* Survival: of
    Soul
Soul Travel, 2, 140, 150, 193
  Ancient Science of. *See*
    ECKANKAR
  and accepting Living ECK
    Master, 141
  beginners in, 149

experiences, 33, 36, 142,
148, 239
misunderstandings about,
145
motives to learn, 138
as phase in ECKANKAR,
145, 147
preparations for, 43
upliftment via, 44
as way to heaven, 137, 139,
162
*Soul Travel 1 — The Illumi-
nated Way,* 240
Sound(s)
of bells, 51, 56
of birds, 56
of buzzing (bees), 12, 13, 29
clicking, 11, 35
of crickets, 29, 43
of ECK, 35, 147
of electrostatic hum, 29,
182
flow of, 148
of flute(s), 12, 13, 29, 43
hearing ECK as, 42, 142,
149, 241
of HU. *See* HU: sound of
of plane(s), 139
as roar of sea, 29
of thunder, 29
of whistle, 43
of wind, 12, 13, 148
of woodwinds, 12
Sound Current, 13, 28, 41, 42.
43, 45, 49, 176, 182, 212,
231
Spartans, 82–83
Spider, 192
Spirit, 154, 232. *See also* ECK;
Holy Spirit
aspects of, 27, 36. *See also*
Light and Sound
being used by, 95, 122, 177
contact with, 50
experiences with, 12
flow of, 238
help from, 127
studying, 12

Spiritual
body, 12. *See also* Body(ies):
Soul
bondage, 220
crib, 109–11
exercises. *See* Spiritual Exercises of ECK
experiences, 37–38, 116
foundation, 50
freedom, 62, 142
growth, 75, 79, 142, 182, 221
hunger, 63
law(s). *See* Law(s): of Spirit
levels. *See* Plane(s): higher;
World(s): God; World(s):
higher
liberation. *See* Liberation,
spiritual
life, 77, 115
maturity, 147
needs, 86
new year, 215, 233
opportunity, 188
polishing, 22
principle(s), 193
reality, 156
realization, 205
revolution, 95
survival. *See* Survival: spiritual
unfoldment. *See* Un-
foldment: spiritual
Spiritual Eye, 11, 35, 42, 44,
51, 82, 106, 139, 146, 169,
238
Spiritual Traveler, 163, 175.
See also Living ECK
Master
Spiritual traveler(s), 33, 34,
121, 175, 225. *See also*
ECK Master(s)
Spiritual Exercises of ECK,
204
children and, 30
and discipline, 127, 222
in discourses, 240
in ECK books, 12
experiences during, 30, 175

265

How to Learn More about ECKANKAR

People want to know the secrets of life and death. In response to this need Sri Harold Klemp, today's spiritual leader of ECKANKAR, and Paul Twitchell, its modern-day founder, have written special monthly discourses which reveal the Spiritual Exercises of ECK—to lead Soul in a direct way to God.

Those who wish to study ECKANKAR can receive these special monthly discourses which give clear, simple instructions for the spiritual exercises. The first annual series of discourses is *The ECK Dream 1 Discourses*. Mailed each month, the discourses will offer insight into your dreams and what they mean to you.

The techniques in these discourses, when practiced twenty minutes a day, are likely to prove survival beyond death. Many have used them as a direct route to Self-Realization, where one learns his mission in life. The next stage, God Consciousness, is the joyful state wherein Soul becomes the spiritual traveler, an agent for God. The underlying principle one learns is this: Soul exists because God loves It.

Membership in ECKANKAR includes:

1. Twelve monthly lessons of *The ECK Dream 1 Discourses,* with such titles as: "Dreams—The Bridge to Heaven," "The Dream Master," "How to Interpret Your Dreams," and "Dream Travel to Soul Travel." You may study them alone at home or in a class with others.
2. The *Mystic World,* a quarterly newsletter with a Wisdom Note and articles by the Living ECK Master. In it are also letters and articles from students of ECKANKAR around the world.
3. Special mailings to keep you informed of upcoming ECKANKAR seminars and activities worldwide, new study materials available from ECKANKAR, and more.
4. The opportunity to attend ECK Satsang classes and book discussions with others in your community.
5. Initiation eligibility.
6. Attendance at certain chela meetings at ECK seminars.

How to Find out More

To request membership in ECKANKAR using your credit card (or for a free booklet on membership) call (612) 544-0066 between 8 a.m. and 5 p.m., central time.

Discover How You Can Receive
Spiritual Guidance and Protection

There May Be an
ECKANKAR Study Group near You

ECKANKAR offers a variety of local and international activities for the spiritual seeker. With hundreds of study groups worldwide, ECKANKAR is near you! Many areas have ECKANKAR Centers where you can browse through the books in a quiet, unpressured environment, talk with others who share an interest in this ancient teaching, and attend beginning discussion classes on how to gain the attributes of Soul: wisdom, power, love, and freedom.

Around the world, ECKANKAR study groups offer special one-day or weekend seminars on the basic teachings of ECKANKAR. Check your phone book under **ECKANKAR**, or call **(612) 544-0066** for membership information and the location of the ECKANKAR Center or study group nearest you. Or write **ECKANKAR, Att: Information, P.O. Box 27300, Minneapolis, MN 55427 U.S.A.**

☐ Please send me information on the nearest ECKANKAR discussion or study group in my area.

☐ Please send me more information about membership in ECKANKAR, which includes a twelve-month spiritual study of dreams.

Please type or print clearly   941

Name _____

Street _____ Apt. # _____

City _____ State/Prov. _____

Zip/Postal Code _____ Country _____

(Our policy: Your name and address are held in strict confidence. We do not rent or sell our mailing lists. Nor will anyone call on you. Our purpose is only to show people the ECK way home to God.)